SECRET AMERICA

Merry Christmas!
2010

To Dan

It's been another great year with you guys and I hope next year is even better. I know this book was mass published by "the man" but I thought you would at least get a kick out of it

Misha & Katie
love you!

SECRET AMERICA

THE HIDDEN SYMBOLS, CODES, AND MYSTERIES OF THE UNITED STATES

BARB KARG AND RICK SUTHERLAND

AVON, MASSACHUSETTS

Published by
Adams Media, a division of F+W Media, Inc.
57 Littlefield Street, Avon, MA 02322. U.S.A.
www.adamsmedia.com

Contains material adapted and abridged from *The Everything® Freemasons
Book*, by John K. Young and Barb Karg, copyright © 2006 by F+W Media, Inc.,
ISBN 10: 1-59869-059-0, ISBN 13: 978-1-59869-059-0; *The Everything® Kabbalah Book*, by Mark Elber, copyright © 2006 by F+W Media, Inc., ISBN 10:
1-59337-546-8, ISBN 13: 978-1-59337-546-1; *The Everything® Philosophy Book*,
by James Mannion, copyright © 2002 by F+W Media, Inc., ISBN 10: 1-58062-
644-0, ISBN 13: 978-1-58062-644-6; and *The Skeptic's Guide to Conspiracies*, by
Monte Cook, copyright © 2009 by F+W Media, Inc., ISBN 10: 1-60550-113-1,
ISBN 13: 978-1-60550-113-0.

ISBN 10: 1-4405-0553-5
ISBN 13: 978-1-4405-0553-9
eISBN 10: 1-4405-0723-6
eISBN 13: 978-1-4405-0723-6

Printed in the United States of America.

10   9   8   7   6   5   4   3   2   1

Library of Congress Cataloging-in-Publication Data
is available from the publisher.

This publication is designed to provide accurate and authoritative information
with regard to the subject matter covered. It is sold with the understanding that
the publisher is not engaged in rendering legal, accounting, or other professional
advice. If legal advice or other expert assistance is required, the services of a com-
petent professional person should be sought.

—From a *Declaration of Principles* jointly adopted by a Committee of the
American Bar Association and a Committee of Publishers and Associations

Many of the designations used by manufacturers and sellers to distinguish their
product are claimed as trademarks. Where those designations appear in this book
and Adams Media was aware of a trademark claim, the designations have been
printed with initial capital letters.

*This book is available at quantity discounts for bulk purchases.
For information, please call 1-800-289-0963.*

CONTENTS

PART ONE

AMERICA'S SECRET HERITAGE

*"American Democracy is part
of a Universal Plan."*

—Manly P. Hall

Sure, we all know that America is the world's greatest republic, heralded as the land of the free and the home of the brave. But America is—and has been for thousands of years—considered by the ancient philosophers, our founding fathers, and modern pundits alike to be much, much more. Known by many arcane names—the New Atlantis, Utopia, even the Holy Grail—our nation is built on the ideas and ideologies of an amazing variety of religions, mystical traditions, and philosophies.

From Pythagoras to the pyramids, astrology to the Illuminati, every aspect of our democracy bears evidence of these hidden influences. Let's take a closer look at our esoteric heritage and the ancient and obscure institutions that inform it. As we'll see, every influence, both ancient and modern, usually relates to Freemasonry, sooner or later, one way or another.

CHAPTER 1

YES, VIRGINIA, THERE IS A SECRET AMERICA

If there is one facet of the human experience that's attained the status of a very guilty American pleasure, it's our complete and unabashed passion for discovering the answers to secrets of any and every variety. While we all have our own fiercely protected personal secrets, there's nothing that piques our inherently curious national psyche quite so instantly as seeing or hearing these words: *covert, confidential, classified,* or *secret.*

Culturally Intrigued

In American culture, we're virtually consumed by a fervent need to know the truth; just exactly what is going on out there? American author Dan Brown's phenomenally bestselling works *The Da Vinci Code* and most recently *The Lost Symbol* exemplify by their very success our zeal for unraveling the riddles of American history and the effects they have on us today. Among our most widely read publications, magazines such as *People* and *Us* delve into the lives and habits of the famous "beautiful people," the formerly famous but fallen from grace, and the far more infamous doings of ne'er-do-wells and outright criminals for the singular purpose of exposing their secrets. On the Internet, the wildly popular tell-all anonymous website, *www.postsecret.com*, ranks at number 3,200 on the web's most regularly visited sites. That's 3,200 out of a list of billions.

FREEDOM AND INFORMATION

Interestingly, one of the primary reasons we're so determined to delve into the mysterious side of life, be it religious, political, geographical, or historical in nature, is the simple fact that we have the basic freedoms to do so. While conspiracy theorists offer dire warnings of the dangers of getting too close to jealously guarded secrets and activities protected by various covert government agencies, the reality is that for the vast majority of us, we have every right to fearlessly poke into the dimmest corners of the shadowy world of Secret America.

One of the most ironic twists in our determination to ferret out the truth centers quite directly on the broad influence that the fraternal order of Freemasons has had on our way of life and our various opinions about who is really pulling the national puppet strings. Although Freemasonry has proved to be the mother lode of vast and intricately complicated conspiratorial theories, the tenets of Freemasonry have also arguably provided the cornerstones of American religious freedoms, democracy, and symbiotic coexistence (see Chapter 5).

BORN TO SECRECY

One of America's most basic, and perhaps treasured, historical heritages is that this nation was created in virtual secrecy. Nearly 250 years ago the Founding Fathers met, conspired, plotted, planned, and then pulled the rug from beneath the British monarchy. During the earliest stages of the American Revolutionary War for independence in 1776, British military leaders made bets with one another as to which one would lead the battle to crush these rebellious upstarts, and how many months it would take to do it. By the time the Treaty of Paris was signed in 1783, Great Britain had taken a whipping that resounded throughout the world, and a new nation rejoiced. All of this successful—and rather shocking—political upheaval and rebirth was based on secrecy and conspiracy, and even today we still get a bit tingly at the very audacity and courage of our brilliantly furtive forefathers.

Despite the relatively young age of the United States, we've inherited through the generations a virtual cornucopia of curiosities, some of which border on the downright diabolical. For example, do the streets and intersections of Washington, D.C., symbolize undisclosed Satanic beliefs of our forefathers? Do the words and phrasings of the U.S. Constitution convey the tenets of some nefarious Masonic plot? Is the Great Seal of the United States a treasured national icon, or does it instead signify a dastardly determination to inflict a "New World Order" on a blissfully unobservant society? That's some pretty heady stuff for any population to ponder.

THE TRUTH IS CLOSER THAN YOU KNOW

It would seem only appropriate to quote the immortal words of modern-day *X-Files* sage Fox Mulder when he asserts, "The truth *is* out there." That is precisely what we seek to explore in this mysterious little tome. What you're certain to find intriguing is what scholars, historians, and experts have to say about America's secrets and mysteries and what conspiracy theorists also surmise. What we endeavor to do is present to you divergent points of view so that you'll have a well-informed background of the secrets, lies, enigmas, and mysteries that all of us are so terminally curious about. Do the Illuminati really exist? Who was the mysterious man behind the Georgia Guidestones, sometimes called "America's Stonehenge"?

Throughout the following chapters, we'll explore the concepts of national secrets, plots, and schemes, which are as old as mankind and are continually revived, refined, and redistributed—often with seemingly convincing evidence. Did George Washington, a renowned Freemason in his day, place his faith for the future of his young country in the mysterious "Great Architect"? Surprisingly, the answer is affirmative. Is the U.S. one-dollar bill rife with hidden Masonic symbolism? Maybe. Are there dozens of secretive organizations planning the destiny of the United States? Absolutely.

A Fog of Fact and Fiction

Above all, it must be said that the secrets and mysteries of our beloved nation are mired in a swirling fog of fact, fiction, controversy, supposition, flat-out untruths, and all measure of wild conspiracy theories. Of course, that's what makes the subject of American secrecy so enticing, and gives us the perfect opportunity to provide you with the best information possible on some of the most prominent and obscure American mysteries from the political to the paranormal. Considering the U.S. is still in its infancy—only two centuries old—it's amazing how many mysteries have been amassed, a fact that clearly makes us a nation of clandestine overachievers!

The tools to discover the truth *are* out there, and the world of secrecy truly is our own clandestine oyster to open. That said, let's take a peek inside Chapter 2 and delve into the deepest recesses of our religious legacies. They go back further than you may think.

CHAPTER 2

THE SECRET RELIGIONS OF AMERICA

If you think of America as a Christian nation, think again. What we think of as All-American symbols, philosophy, and theology boasts a host of ancient and esoteric influences—from the gods and goddesses of Ancient Greece to the mystical revelations of the Judaic discipline known as the Kabbalah. Let's take a look at these religions and their impact on us today and through the ages.

One Nation under One God: Atenism

The first monotheistic religion was not Judaism, as many people believe. It was actually Aten, an ancient religion founded by an Egyptian pharaoh who may have also been the first democrat.

AKHENATEN: THE FIRST REAL AMERICAN?

Some believe that the first man to stand up for democracy was an ancient king named Amen-Hotep IV, Pharaoh of Egypt (1370–1353 BCE). This Pharaoh of the Eighteenth Dynasty rejected the religion of his day and formed the monotheistic religion Atenism. He changed his name to Akhenaten, meaning "servant of Aten," and overturned the existing polytheistic religion in favor of worshiping Aten, the Father represented by a solar disk, who is to his people as "the sun is to the stars." The sun to the Egyptians represented the foundation of life itself, the symbol of Light, Truth, and Joy. Akhenaten led his kingdom with surprisingly tolerant policies based on peace and relative equality. The art of the time, which had previously depicted pharaohs in only formal and restricted poses, showed Akhenaten at home with his wife Nefertiti and their children.

FROM AKHENATEN TO AMERICA

The Rosicrucian Ancient and Mystical Order of the Rosy Cross, headquartered in San Jose, California, claims Akhenaten as its founder.

The Mystery Schools of Ancient Egypt

In antiquity, the word *mystery* referred to a special *gnosis,* a secret wisdom. *Mystery* itself comes from the Greek *mysterios,* meaning secret. Thousands of years ago in ancient Egypt, select bodies or schools were formed to explore the mysteries of life and learn the fiercely guarded secrets of this hidden wisdom, which was verbally transmitted from teacher to student.

In ancient days, the schools met in secluded chambers in magnificent old temples to initiate select candidates into the great mysteries. Later their mystical studies assumed a more closed character and were held exclusively in temples constructed for that purpose.

BACK TO EGYPT

Pharaoh Thutmose III, who ruled Egypt from 1500 to 1447 BCE, organized the first esoteric school of initiates founded upon principles and methods that are still followed today. Decades later, Akhenaten was so inspired by the mystery teachings that, as we've seen, he spun Egypt's religion and philosophy into a completely new direction.

THE MYSTERIES GROW

Those ancient mystery schools flourished all across Asia, the Middle East, and Greece. The mysteries honored the local gods and goddesses. From Osiris and Isis of Egypt to Persephone and Dionysius of Greece, the stories shared the same themes of life, death, and rebirth. The stories have been passed down through the millennia and today are common knowledge, but the secret rites and rituals that allowed initiates to experience that life, death, and rebirth for themselves remain hidden. These rites and rituals—and their promise of enlightenment—have been wrapped in story and symbolism and kept close by secret societies ever since.

THE PHARAOH LIVES IN CENTRAL PARK

It's called Cleopatra's Needle, but in fact the seventy-one-foot, 244-ton obelisk in New York's Central Park was one of many built by Pharaoh Thutmose III during his reign. Two other "needles" stand in London and Paris, also built by Thutmose. When the obelisk was put in place in 1881, a Freemason Grand Master, Jesse B. Anthony, laid the cornerstone with a full Masonic ceremony.

IT'S ALL GREEK TO ME

Many of the most renowned Classical philosophers—Thales, Pythagoras, and the Roman philosopher Plotinus, among others—journeyed to Egypt and were initiated into the mystery schools, then returned home to share their wisdom. These first written records of the mysteries formed the basis of the knowledge of many of the secret societies—from the Rosicrucian Order to the Freemasons.

During the Carolingian Empire (742–814), the French scholar Arnaud introduced the mystical teachings into France, and from there they spread through much of Western Europe. Throughout medieval Europe, mystical knowledge was often necessarily couched in symbolism or disguised and hidden in the love songs of troubadours, the formularies of alchemists, the symbolical system known as the Qabala, and the rituals of Orders of Knighthood.

LONG LIVE ANCIENT MYSTERIES

The Ancient Mysteries refer to a body of secret knowledge that enables its practitioners to tap into their true potential, to access those parts of their brains that have gone unused. This knowledge was only passed to enlightened Adepts who were worthy of the knowledge and who pledged to keep it from becoming common knowledge where it might have been misused by the uninitiated. Almost every ancient society believed that an elite group of spiritual seekers had access to ancient knowledge that they could then use to obtain mystical or god-like powers. In each society, elite members would have to be worthy of being trusted with these Ancient Mysteries and would go through an initiation process to join the elite group.

While much of medieval Europe lay in darkness, the highly advanced Arab civilization preserved and protected its mystical teachings through texts translated directly from the great libraries of the ancient world, such as Egypt's Alexandria Library. The contents of these philosophy, medicine, mathematics, and alchemy texts were later transmitted to Europe by way of the Arabs.

The Eleusinian Mysteries

The most famous—even infamous—of the Ancient Mysteries may be the Eleusinian Mysteries, which date back to 1600

BCE. These initiation ceremonies, which celebrated Demeter, her daughter Persephone, and the coming of Spring after Winter, flourished for more than 2,000 years, spreading all the way to Rome. Luminaries from Plato to Cicero lauded the power and beauty of the Mysteries, which in the tradition of these ceremonies offered the promise of enlightenment, transformation, and—ultimately—immortality. This promise was acted out in three stages of consciousness:

1. *Dromena*, the things done
2. *Legomena*, the things said
3. *Deiknymena*, the things shown

This elevation of consciousness is the reward that awaits participants in these Mysteries.

SEX, DRUGS, AND SPRING ROLLS AROUND

Although all initiates were sworn to a secrecy rarely breached, later reports by Christians, who considered themselves not bound to such oaths, as well as scholarly and archeological discoveries have led some scholars to believe that the Eleusinian Mysteries included the consumption of psychoactive agents. This would certainly help explain the rapidly altered states of consciousness experienced by those participants in the Mysteries. There is also some evidence that the ceremonies included "venerated congress of the hierophant with the priestess," at least according to the appalled fourth-century bishop Asterius. No surprise there, since the Eleusinian Mysteries were a celebration of the cycle of life, as symbolized by the changing seasons. According to myth, Persephone, daughter of Demeter, the goddess of crops, was abducted by Hades, lord of the Underworld. Distraught, Demeter wandered the Earth, searching for her daughter. Crops withered and died, and the world became a cold and bleak place. At last, Zeus persuaded Hades to reunite Persephone with her mother. However, the daughter had eaten six pomegranate seeds in the Underworld, and thus her return could only be temporary. During the spring and summer she lives above ground, and Demeter, in her joy, permits vegetation and crops to flourish. Then, for six months, Persephone must return to the Underworld, and her mother mourns her absence, plunging the world into winter.

WHAT REMAINS

The initiates into the Eleusinian Mysteries were sworn to secrecy under penalty of death. So the Eleusinian Mysteries remain for the most part mysterious. That said, the transformation of consciousness and the promise of immortality are as relevant today as they were thousands of years ago. And the secret societies that insist they are the torchbearers of this ancient wisdom may be our keys to divinity.

THE COMING APOCALYPSE

The word *apocalypse* means to unveil or to reveal. One could interpret the Book of Revelation to mean that there will be a reveal-ation, the unveiling of great wisdom and truths that will bring an end to the world as we know it.

Pythagoras: God Is in the Numbers

"Know thyself."

—Pythagoras

Sure, you know the ancient Greek mathematician Pythagoras gave us the Pythagorean theorem we all learned in high school, but Pythagoras was also a man of faith who started his own cult inspired by the Ancient Mysteries. His disciples were sworn to secrecy on pain of death. He also believed in reincarnation, and his followers were vegetarians.

Rather than suggest that the basic stuff of reality was an element of nature, Pythagoras proposed that life was a numbers game. He taught that everything could be explained through mathematical theorems and formulae.

GET A CLUE!

The English occultist and mathematician John Dee created a magical script, which consisted of Pythagorean geometry and mathematical symbols, that was later adopted by a number of fraternities to code secrets. «

THE MAGIC SQUARE

The Pythagoreans may have a point in that there's something magical about numbers and what they can do. Believed to have originated in China, India, and Arabia more than 4,000 years ago, magic squares are an example of mathematical magic.

Magic squares consist of a series of numbers in a grid in which all the numbers in each row, column, and diagonal add up to the same number, known as "the magic constant." They can be constructed from 3 x 3 upwards. For each size, the constant remains fixed. For a 3 x 3, it is 15; for a 4 x 4 is it 34; and so on. For a 3 x 3, there is only one conceivable arrangement; for a 4 x 4, there are 880 possibilities. For example, here's a simple 3 x 3 magic square:

2	7	6
9	5	1
4	3	8

In this example, all the numbers in all the columns add up to 15. The Renaissance artist Albrecht Dürer, who could never resist showing off his own cleverness, created a magic square in his engraving *Melencholia*, seen on the pillar behind the central figure. In Dürer's square, not only do the rows, columns, and diagonals equal 34, but so do the 2 x 2 squares in each of the four corners and the 2 x 2 square at the center of the grid. In his grid, the two middle numbers in the bottom rows (15 and 14) are the date the engraving was produced, while the numbers on either side (4 and 1) are a shortcut for his name (4 = D and 1 = A).

Here is Dürer's square.

16	3	2	13
5	10	11	8
9	6	7	12
4	15	14	1

In this square, each column as well as each diagonal adds up to 34. In addition, each of the 2 x 2 squares that form the four quadrants of the larger square also add up to 34. The four small squares at the corners of the large square (16, 13, 1, 4) add up to . . . you guessed it! 34.

THE SYMBOLISM OF NUMBERS

Numbers have a multiplicity of meaning in mythology:

TWO: Duality (the sun and the moon; men and women; night and day; light and darkness; hot and cold; yin and yang)

THREE: The trilogy of life (mind, body, spirit; birth, life, death; past, present, future; beginning, middle, end)

FOUR: Stability and the grounded and contained nature of all things (four seasons; four directions; four elements; four cycles of the moon)

SEVEN: The relationship between man and god (the world was created in seven days; there are seven deadly sins; seven heavens; seven stages of initiation)

EIGHT: Eternity (ecliptic or projection of the path of the sun through the Zodiac; for Freemasons the path of initiation)

THIRTEEN: Despite some negative connotations for the number 13, perhaps because Judas Iscariot was the thirteenth person to arrive at the Last Supper, it can also have positive symbolism. There are thirteen lunar months in the year (with a small error), which led the Maya and the Hebrews to consider 13 as auspicious. In medieval theology, 13 reduces to 10 + 3, which equals the ten commandments plus the trinity, giving the number its positive aspects.

THE TETRACTYS

In addition to Magic Squares, the Pythagoreans were interested in something called the Tetractys. This is ten points or dots arranged in the shape of a pyramid, the base of the pyramid being four points in a row.

GET A CLUE!

According to Dan Brown's novel *The Lost Symbol,* the legendary Masonic pyramid atop the George Washington Monument is described as enormous, with a tip forged of solid gold. Without its tip, it becomes an unfinished pyramid symbolizing that man's quest to rise to his full potential is constantly a work in progress. This is the symbol on our dollar bill, representing our unfulfilled destiny and the work yet to be done.«

Pythagoras's followers believed the Tetractys had mystical powers and represented the mathematical nature of reality. The apex of the pyramid was a singularity or zero dimensions; the next layer was a line between two points (one dimension); the third was a flat triangle shape of width and breadth but no height (two dimensions); while the fourth layer introduced the three-dimensional world in which we live.

Some have said that the Tetractys influenced Kabbalist writings. Others suggest that it's connected to the mystical rite of Tarot cards. In any case, it shows the importance the image of the pyramid played in early Greek thought.

GET A CLUE!

Gold and silver are very powerful symbols. American currency was, for many years on the Gold Standard, though in 1896 orator William Jennings Bryan fulminated against it, crying out, "You shall not crucify mankind upon a cross of gold!"

The ancients considered gold magical. It has also been an almost universal symbol of the sun, representing illumination and immortality. Ancient Egyptians believed that gold held tangible presence of the gods; Aztecs viewed gold as the sun god's excrement; Chinese Taoists viewed it as the essence of heaven.

Silver typically represents the moon or feminine energy. It is associated with virginity, and with being silver-tongued or eloquent. Christians bestowed a negative connotation based on the connection of thirty pieces of silver paid to Judas for Christ's betrayal. That did not, however, stop the casting of many beautiful silver Christian ornaments.«

Hermetism: We Are All Connected

"As above, so below."

—*The Emerald Tablet*, Hermes Trismegistus

The Emerald Tablet was one of the works found in the *Hermetica*, a set of religious and philosophical writings that came to light in Egypt in the second century. These works are attributed to Hermes Trismegistus, who some believe was a contemporary of Moses. Others believe he represents the fusion of the Egyptian god Thoth and the Greek god Hermes, who shared associations with magic, medicine, prophecy, and the Moon.

GEORGE WASHINGTON'S APRON

When George Washington laid the cornerstone of the Capitol building on September 18, 1793, in full Masonic regalia, he was wearing an apron embroidered by Madame Lafayette. On this apron were two columns representing the pillars from the Temple of Solomon. According to legend, the pillars were lost after the Flood—and years afterward, Pythagoras found one, and Hermes Trismegistus found the other.

Hermetics believed that man was born of God and that with proper study, meditation, and initiation, people could return to that divine state—becoming one with God and with all things.

This belief is echoed in the Bible, and in Gnosticism, an early form of Christian mysticism. This view was later deemed heresy by the Catholic Church, and the Hermeticists were largely driven underground for hundreds of years. They re-emerged during the Renaissance, which ushered in a new interest in Hermeticism—and its cultural influences are still seen today, from the Rosicrucians to *The Lost Symbol*.

┌─────────────────── GET A CLUE! ───────────────────┐

Often Freemasons will have a meditation room or sacred space where they can seek spiritual sanctuary, privacy for contemplation. Chambers of reflection are common in Masonic lodges, but some may also set aside a space in their homes.

Some Masons will inscribe the word *Vitriol* on a wall in their Chamber of Reflection. It's a Latin acronym for the Masonic meditative mantra: *Visita interiora terrae, rectificando invenies occultum lapidem.* Visit the interior of the earth, and by rectifying, you will find the hidden stone.«

└──┘

THE OCCULTISM CONNECTION

The origins of Western occultism can be traced back to the Hermetica texts, which date back to the first century AD. These texts, which are dialogues between various gods, embrace the duality of matter and spirit and the idea that man can achieve salvation through knowledge rather than faith. The Hermetica belief system taught that man is an immortal spirit captured in a mortal body and that man could achieve liberation, or reunion with God, by learning to understand his own nature.

THE PHILOSOPHER'S STONE

The Philosopher's Stone is a mysterious object that alchemists believed could turn base metals such as lead into gold. Scientist and alchemist Sir Isaac Newton believed that the secret to the Philosopher's Stone was in *The Emerald Tablet.* Newton translated the work into English himself from the Latin Tabula Smaragdina, hoping to decode its secrets. Alchemists believed that the red powder from the Philosopher's Stone was the key ingredient needed to turn lead into gold.

Based on Greek and Egyptian Hermetic literature, occult-ist initiates always take a journey governed by medieval plane-tary or zodiacal symbols. The understanding of these symbols, however, is never explained to the neophyte. Instead the understanding must come from within the person making the journey and interpreting the symbols in relation to his or her unique journey.

Hermetic beliefs influenced the authors of the Bible. For instance, the Hermetic liturgy reads, "I in thee and thou in me." In the Gospel According to John 17:21 we find, "Thou, Father, art in me and I in thee."

Light and Truth: Mithraism

From the first through the fourth century AD there was one dominant religion on the European continent, a "mystery" cult called Mithraism. For more than two centuries this reli-gion proved to be a powerful rival to Christianity. Throughout Europe and Asia, Mithras was called by many names, but he is commonly known as the Persian god of light and truth, who is often associated with the sun.

According to legend, Mithras came down to Earth to gather his followers into an army. In a cave, he engaged in a battle against a fierce bull, which took the physical form of the Spirit of All Evil. After defeating the bull, Mithras returned to the heavens to judge the dead and lead the righteous. In Mithraic art, he is usually shown sitting atop a bull, a knife in hand, often depicted with other animals. (In other depictions, Mithras is sometimes shown with the god of the Sun.)

Mithraism was an exclusive religion (that is, its followers did not believe in other religions), replete with symbolism, ritual, and rich ties to the astronomical world. Ironically, the Christians of the day compared Mithraism to their own doc-trines and, having judged them to be similar, deduced that the

Mithraics were a religion created by Satan for the purpose of leading souls astray.

So hated were the Mithraics by the Christians that when the latter finally overpowered the cult, they annihilated everything associated with the religion, in fact rebuilding on the destroyed shrines. Only a few underground shrines survived and still exist in Europe.

TWO OF A KIND

Curiously, Mithraism and Freemasonry seem to have a lot in common. Like the Freemasons, the Mithraic cult was comprised solely of men. While Freemasons have three main degrees or levels of entry, Mithraism's followers separated into seven "grades." Each of these grades had a symbolic ceremony in which initiates spoke vows, were baptized, and continued on to the next grade. Each level imparted more knowledge to followers and brought them a step closer to Mithras. It has been speculated that these practices were very much in line with the rituals and ceremonies of Masonry.

Mithraics gathered in a cavern-shaped meeting place called a *mithreum* in deference to Mithras's legendary cave battle with the formidable bull. Mithreums, like Masonic lodges, had a president and a full range of presiding officers. Its membership was greatly varied in terms of class, but both slaves and men of liberty were afforded the same considerations and entrusted duties of equal accord.

SYMBOLIC SYMMETRY

Symbolism was of great importance to the Mithraics, as they never recorded in writing any of their secrets or rituals. Freemasonry shares many of these common symbols—the sun, moon, stars, globes, and a ladder with seven rungs that symbolizes the ascension of a candidate to higher degrees. This is much like the seven-rung ladder used in Craft rituals.

The astronomical symbols are of particular interest. In Mithraism, the seven grades are symbolic of the seven planets (Mercury, Venus, Mars, Jupiter, Saturn, and the sun and moon). The bull Mithras slays is representative of Taurus, and the other animals often shown with him translate to other signs of the zodiac and, subsequently, the constellations. Ancients looked to the stars and sun in order to track the equinoxes and summer and winter solstices. In addition to his other heavenly duties, Mithras oversaw the changing of the seasons and heaven's movement. His slaying of the bull denotes the coming equinox.

Another commonality between Mithraism and Freemasonry is the symbolic death used in their respective rituals. The Mithraics used the legend of Mithras slaying the bull and representations of death and resurrection in their ceremonies, much the same way the Freemasons use the Legend of Hiram Abiff (see Chapter 4).

While much time and effort has been devoted to the study of these two disciplines, no one has been able to make a definitive connection between them. The possibility that Freemasonry descended from Mithraism is fascinating, but it remains a speculation.

Bullish on America
Here are some of the clues that reveal the cultural impact of the Mithraic mystery cult on our culture and society:

- Wall Street's Bull Market
- The "Eye of Taurus" on the Great American Seal
- George Washington Masonic Memorial
- The Seven Steps of Freemasonry
- The Seven Liberal Arts of Freemasonry

Judaism and the Temple of Solomon

The influence of the Judeo-Christian tradition on the United States has never been in doubt—but the secret impact of Judaism on America is less often acknowledged. The Freemasons trace the origins of their Craft back to King Solomon—and this reveals itself in myriad ways.

GET A CLUE!

A system using symbols to invoke spirits that man can use to attain self-knowledge and ultimately a full spiritual evolution is known as The Key of Solomon from the fourteenth-century book from which it's derived. The book was quite possibly influenced by Kabbalistic rituals, which may have had their origins in magical practices of Greek and Rome. The practitioner dons special garments and draws or stands upon a mandala-like symbol representing his body, mind, and soul. To his right or left is a triangular shape. Through a series of complex invocations, he is able to draw spirits to him and thus liberate his own soul. «

One of Freemasonry's alleged origins dates back to the building of Solomon's Temple in Jerusalem from 970 to 931 BCE. Considered by both the Bible and the Torah as the first official temple in the Holy City, it was a massive undertaking that required thousands of men, enormous resources, and the skills of many master craftsmen.

It is said that King Solomon, son of David and Bathsheba, was in dire need of a master artisan and consulted one of his friends, Hiram, the king of Tyre, to see if he could offer such a man to work on the great temple. Eager to help build a house of God, the Tyrian king dispatched his master workman, a skilled artist named Hiram Abiff. Abiff, according to some legends, was not only a great architect but he became the lover of Bathsheba. Out of jealousy, Solomon connived at his murder by three ruffians, an event that has passed into Masonic legend. We'll discuss this more in a later chapter.

SOLOMON'S QUARRIES

Also known as Zedekiah's Cave, Solomon's Quarries is a five-acre underground meleke limestone quarry that runs the length of five city blocks under the Muslim Quarter of the Old City of Jerusalem. It was carved over a period of several thousand years and is a remnant of the biggest quarry in Jerusalem, having once stretched all the way from Jeremiah's Grotto and the Garden Tomb—according to Protestant tradition the site of Jesus' burial—to the walls of the Old City. The Freemasons of Israel hold an annual ceremony in Zedekiah's Cave, and they consider it one of the most revered sites in their history. (Masonic ritual claims that King Solomon was their first Grand Master, and some Freemasons feel that the cave is definitely Solomon's Quarry.)

Since the 1860s, Israeli Freemasons have been holding ceremonies in the cave. From the days of the British Mandate in the 1920s, the cave was used for the ceremony of Mark Master Masons. Although this practice was temporarily suspended between the years 1948 and 1968, the impressive ceremony of the consecration of the Supreme Grand Royal Arch Chapter of the State of Israel was commenced again in the spring of 1969, and ever since then the Mark degree has been performed in the caves on the average of once a year.

Solomon Lives On in America

Evidence of King Solomon's faith and wisdom are all around us, in both our past and our present as a nation.

- Benjamin Franklin edited and printed James Anderson's *The Constitutions of the Free-Masons,* the first book of

Masonic rituals and secrets to be published in America, which featured a detailed description of the Temple of Solomon.

- American Masonic rituals are inspired by Hiram Abiff and the Temple of Solomon.
- The Seal of Solomon, also known as the Star of David, is a six-pointed star found on every U.S. dollar bill.

Kabbalism

Just as Christianity has had Gnosticism, a body of secret, forbidden knowledge within the context of the Christian faith, so Judaism has had the Kabbalah. (A roughly similar tradition, Sufism, exists in Islam.)

Kabbalism uses the Torah as a tool to explore deeper issues of humans' understanding of themselves and their place in the universe. While it is difficult to know the historical origins of Kabbalism with absolute certainty, discovered texts indicate that it surfaced in the late 1100s in southern France in the area of Provence and soon spread to northern Spain.

Much of Kabbalistic literature has been transmitted orally rather than through print. Many Kabbalistic texts are heavily encoded with symbolic language. They are also often written with many thoughts unfinished. Quotations are given in fragments, just enough to make them recognizable to those familiar with the traditional sources.

Kabbalists hope to use various techniques to break out of conventional ways of seeing the world. Our standard way of perceiving the world is by seeing with "our physical eyes" instead of seeing with our "spiritual eyes." Viewing the world using our "spiritual eyes" is an important goal for Kabbalists.

99 PERCENT CLUELESS

According to the Kabbalah Centre in Los Angeles, what we as unenlightened humans perceive as reality in truth represents only 1 percent of reality. By studying the Kabbalah, we can access the ancient wisdom that allows us to understand the other 99 percent.

The Kabbalah in La La Land

The mysteries of the Kabbalah are as sought after today as they were 2,000 years ago. Celebrities of every denomination have made the mystical Jewish tradition a chic course of study, particularly at the famous—some would say infamous—Kabbalah Centre in Los Angeles. The beautiful people known to have associated with the Centre include:

- Lindsay Lohan
- Roseanne Barr
- Sandra Bernhard
- Ashton Kutcher
- Demi Moore
- Mick Jagger
- Jerry Hall
- Lucy Liu
- Rosie O'Donnell
- Naomi Campbell
- Donna Karan
- Britney Spears
- David and Victoria Beckham
- Paris Hilton
- Nicole Richie
- Zac Efron

The Wisdom of the Ages ... Not Quite Lost to Antiquity

All of these traditions—the sources of the Ancient Mysteries and wisdom—could have been lost forever when Rome fell and the Dark Ages settled over Europe. But thanks to such zealous groups as the Illuminati, the Knights Templar, and the Rosicrucians, some of the answers to man's greatest questions have survived in one form or another. And remnants of them survive to the present day in America. In the next chapter, we'll examine those secret societies dedicated to the preservation of the Ancient Mysteries, no matter what the cost.

CHAPTER 3
THE SECRET HISTORY
OF AMERICA

All of the adepts, philosophers, prophets, and scholars from ancient to modern times are united in their unrelenting search for truth, wisdom, and—ultimately—the divine. However disparate, these groups share one goal: to acquire and protect the knowledge needed to make the world a sacred place of equality and enlightenment for all.

This quest has made for some interesting history on the way to the United States of America as we know her today.

The 1776 Illuminati

The same year that our nation was born, a shadowy group called the Bavarian Illuminati was born—and some would say that it's no coincidence.

One of the grander conspiracies of the past, present, and future is the concept that a small group of powerful men ultimately rule the world. These men comprise what in the broadest term is known as the Illuminati, or enlightened ones. Many have, no doubt, heard the term before, as this group is often featured in film and in literature, often in shady circumstances and focused on some evil purpose.

There are a number of exclusive clubs comprised of rich and powerful men in our country today that seem to model themselves on the Bavarian Illuminati—from the Trilateral Commission to the Skull and Bones Club (see Chapter 12).

AN UPSTART MASON "ENLIGHTENS" US

Adam Weishaupt was born in 1748 in the German town of Ingolstadt. Educated by Jesuits, he went on to become a professor of Canon Law at the University of Ingolstadt in 1775. Weishaupt immediately had trouble: his views were radical and offensive to the clergy. He condemned bigotry and intolerance and challenged clerical superstitions. He then assembled a group of bright young men and set about creating a private party of opposition within the University. Meeting in secret, Weishaupt introduced his philosophies and liberalism to the group, which marked the beginning of the Order of the Illuminati or "Enlightened Ones," commonly called the Bavarian Illuminati.

On May 1, 1776, Weishaupt and his collaborator, German Freemason Baron Adolph von Knigge, officially founded the Bavarian Illuminati, whose heady aim was to overthrow the Roman Catholic Church, defeat all governments, and eventually rule the world. The plan involved both secrecy and subterfuge, with conspiracy mixed in for good measure. Starting with only five members, the group came to have more than 2,500 members, many of whom were alleged to be Masons or former Masons. It must be said that at the time of the Illuminati's founding, Weishaupt was not a member of the Brotherhood, and his possible initiation is in dispute.

ILLUMINATORS EVERYWHERE

The Bavarian Illuminati wasn't the first group of organized "enlightened" individuals. The Alumbrados of Spain were a mystical sect of reformed Jesuits and Franciscans often cited as Illuminati—most likely because their name means *illuminated* in English. Alumbrados were practitioners of a mystical form of Christianity in Spain during the fifteenth and sixteenth centuries who became suspect during the Inquisition because they retained some of their old practices. Also, the French Illuminés of Avignon, formed in 1770, later became the "Academy of True Masons."

Weishaupt organized the Illuminati into cells. Small groups of secretive agents worked together but didn't know who the members of the other cells were or where the leader could be found. Weishaupt's idea was that the Illuminati cells would spread throughout the world, infiltrating governments and manipulating them—including the United States.

THE ILLUMINATED STATES OF AMERICA

A Scottish Mason named John Robison claimed to have rejected an offer to join the Illuminati, and in 1789 he wrote a book about it called *Proofs of a Conspiracy*. He noted, "An association has been formed for the express purposes of rooting out all the religious establishments and overturning all existing governments . . . the leaders would rule the World with uncontrollable power, while all the rest would be employed as tools of the ambition of their unknown superiors." George Washington got a copy of the book and said that he knew that there were Illuminati cells in America and that they had "diabolical tenets."

But was Washington a secret member of the Illuminati himself? Was his response to Robison's book a clever ruse to throw the Scottish author and others off the trail? Because the American Revolution (and perhaps even more so, the French Revolution) could easily be seen as the result of Illuminati manipulation. In each conflict, a powerful monarch is defeated and a land of religious freedom is created.

Perhaps the creation of the United States itself was an Illuminati action: The Illuminated States of America. Or a means to an even greater end—an illuminated planet.

WEISHAUPT AND WASHINGTON: TWINS SEPARATED AT BIRTH?

By many contemporary accounts, Weishaupt and George Washington were dead ringers. Some on the wilder shores of conspiracy theory have suggested that in fact they *were* the same person. Washington secretly went to Europe and disappeared, and his place in America was taken by Weishaupt.

ONE SECRET SOCIETY LEADS TO ANOTHER . . .

The mere whisper of the word *secret* in relation to Freemasonry is enough for conspiracy theorists to speculate that the Brotherhood is an arm of the Illuminati or that, in fact, the Illuminati evolved from Freemasonry. Scholars, historians, and conspiracists alike have plenty of historical fodder from which to draw in regard to the Bavarian connection. There is, in fact, a slim association between Freemasons and the Bavarian Illuminati, and it is that connection that has given rise to strange theories about the Masons as part of various secret Illuminati-like organizations, including the Priory of Sion, the Bilderberg Group, and the Trilateral Commission to name a few (see Chapter 12).

There is no evidence to suggest that Freemasons supported or created the Illuminati, but the structure of the radical free-thinking group is quite similar to Masonic structure. Illuminati members were divided into three classes, they offered obedience, and there were various officers and ascending degrees. Some speculate that the Illuminati had established relationships with various Masonic lodges in Bavaria and that their enlightened membership over ten years reached to more than 4,000.

The political climate in the eighteenth century was one of guarded tolerance toward Freemasonry. Bavaria was a conservative state dominated by aristocracy and the Catholic Church. The growing publicity and controversy surrounding the Illuminati tipped the balance of favor against all secret societies. As one expert tells it, Baron von Knigge ultimately disagreed with the direction Weishaupt was pursuing and broke from the group.

BEWARE THE CELLULOID ILLUMINATI

In the 2001 movie *Lara Croft: Tomb Raider* starring Angelina Jolie, Lara must fight to keep the evil Illuminati from finding an ancient artifact that will give them the power to control the world.

One theory suggests that the Jesuits, who were still powerful despite having been suppressed, set out to destroy Weishaupt and his Enlightened Ones. A royal decree issued in 1784 banned all secret associations from Bavaria. At that point, the Bavarian Illuminati supposedly ceased activity—or went further underground. Weishaupt escaped prosecution, but his ultimate goals became public when his revolutionary-based papers were discovered and printed by the government. What became of Weishaupt is unclear, but his character and ideals are alternately reviled and revered to the present day.

SO "THEY'RE" THE ONES WHO KILLED KENNEDY!

Conspiracy theorists love to link lots of different plots together. Some conjecture that the Illuminati controlled the Freemasons who killed Kennedy in order to cover up the fake moon landing. Another favorite: The CIA *are* the Men in Black who got the technology for the black helicopters from the aliens in Area 51.

America: The New Atlantis

Weishaupt's Illuminati might just have been the first *known* order of the Illuminati. The shadowy group may have existed for far longer. In fact, the Bavarian Illuminati may have just been a distraction to throw interested parties off the trail of the real Illuminati. That's the way Illuminati researchers think—nothing can be trusted.

The real Illuminati may have started before recorded history, or at least before the history that most people are taught in their (Illuminati-controlled) schools. Hailing from the now-lost continent of Atlantis, supposedly the original Illuminati ruled the world, sailing in fantastic ships and using advanced maps. The Atlanteans ruled over the less developed people of the world, and their influence was responsible for many of the ancient wonders, such as the pyramids (hence the Illuminati's preoccupation with them). Doomed due to a quirk of unstable geology, only a few Atlanteans survived the cataclysm that dragged Atlantis beneath the waves. These secretive, superior masters mixed in with the rest of humanity but kept in contact with each other in secret even as they rose to prominence in various disparate cultures around the globe. Today their spiritual—and perhaps biological—descendants rule from the shadows as the Illuminati.

OUR FOUNDING FATHERS FOUND ATLANTIS

Whether it was the original home of the Illuminati or not, interest in the legend of the long-lost Atlantis was revived with the publishing of Sir Francis Bacon's *The New Atlantis* in 1627, a year after the death of its celebrated author. In this utopian fable, Bacon presents a world governed by the Ancient Mysteries. This very influential book helped inspire the founding of the world's oldest scientific institution, the Royal Society, which boasted not only scientists but also alchemists, Kabbalists, astrologers, hermeticists, and adepts among its members. Even more important, *The New Atlantis* gave our founding fathers the blueprint they needed to found their own new nation based on the Ancient Mysteries.

SOLOMON'S HOUSE A.K.A. THE SMITHSONIAN

"This fable My Lord devised to the end that he might exhibit therein, a model or description of a college, instituted or the interpreting of nature, and the producing of great and marvelous works, or the benefit of men; under the name of Solomon's house or the college of the six days work."
—From the Introduction *to The New Atlantis,* written by *Bacon's chaplain William Rawley*

The legend of Atlantis is alive and well in her new American incarnation as manifested in such people, places, and things as:

- The Folger Shakesepeare Library, where a copy of *The New Atlantis* is housed
- The Library of Congress, where Benjamin Franklin, member of the Royal Society, worked
- The Smithsonian Institute, which seems to be exactly what Rawley had in mind

The Priory of Sion: Real or Fiction?

Like the Illuminati, the Priory of Sion is a fascinating study in both history and conspiracy. But whereas the Illuminati are concerned with political control of the world, the Priory of Sion deals with the spiritual side of things. The Priory is especially important because it allegedly connects Jesus Christ, Mary Magdalene, the Medieval Knights Templar, and ultimately Freemasonry courtesy of secret documents and various associations in history. In regard to the Priory, there is no lack of conspiracy theories, which splinter in all directions from the eleventh century to the present.

Its origins as a secret organization are in dispute, some saying the group was founded in the 1950s, others claiming it dates back to the time of the Crusades. The modern Prieure de Sion, or Priory of Sion, was founded by Pierre Plantard in Annemasse, France, in 1956. With a membership of five men, the society claimed it was a continuation of the Ordre de Sion founded by Frenchman Godfrey de Bouillon in 1090. A leader during the Crusades, de Bouillon became the first ruler of the Kingdom of Jerusalem in 1099. It wasn't long after de Bouillon's death that the Knights Templar were officially recognized. Some experts have speculated that it was the Prieure de Sion who created the Knights Templar as their military and administrative order. The name *Prieure de Sion* was allegedly changed in 1188 to the Priory of Sion when its members and the Templars parted company.

THE PRIORY OF SION TAKES ON ROBERT LANGDON

The name *Priory of Sion* may ring a bell because it plays a large role in Dan Brown's bestselling book *The Da Vinci Code*, featuring his intrepid symbolist hero, Robert Langdon. In *The Da Vinci Code*, the Priory and its Grand Master are integral to the storyline involving the Holy Grail.

Down through the ages, goes the theory, the Priory of Sion was a secret society led by such Grand Masters as Leonardo da Vinci, Isaac Newton, Victor Hugo, and Sandro Botticelli. The first Grand Master was Jean de Gisors, who served from 1188 to 1220. If indeed the Priory exists, the list of previous

Grand Masters includes aristocracy, occultists, alchemists, and Freemasons.

THE HIDDEN PARCHMENTS

As mentioned above, Pierre Plantard "re-founded" the Priory of Sinon in 1956. Something of an eccentric (to put it kindly), he became obsessed with "proving" that he was a descendant of the Merovingian line of kings, who in the early Middle Ages had ruled the kingdom of what eventually became France. At some point in the 1960s, Plantard, together with several others associated with the Priory, forged a series of documents that purported to show Plantard was the heir to the Merovingian throne. They planted these documents in Paris's Bibliotheque Nationale, where they were discovered in 1967. These documents came to be known as *Les Dossiers Secrets* and created something of a sensation at the time of their uncovering.

Plantard later confessed that he had, in fact, placed the documents, but he maintained their ancient and mysterious origin. The documents, he said, originated at Rennes-le-Chateau in Languedoc, France, a mysterious church that has long been an intriguing study of scholars and researchers because of its alleged links to the Holy Grail, the Ark of the Covenant, Noah's Ark, and the hidden treasures of Solomon's Temple. The parish priest of the Chateau in the late nineteenth century had been a certain Berenger Saunière, who allegedly discovered four parchments within a hollowed out Visigoth pillar, along with a mysterious treasure. These parchments, which Plantard claimed were the source of *Les Dossiers Secrets*, showed Plantard to be the last surviving Merovingian.

Plantard then added a further twist to the already odd story. He told his friend Gerard de Sède that the documents Saunière had originally uncovered and that were now part of *Les Dossier Secrets* confirmed French folklore that Jesus had in fact evaded death in Palestine and fled to France, where he lived with Mary Magdalene. Their lineage resulted in the Merovingian dynasty. The Holy Grail, Plantard asserted—which most scholars had identified as the cup that caught Jesus' blood as he hung dying on the cross at Calvary—was not a literal object. Plantard asserted that rather than a "grail" or cup, the true description was *San Greal*. In French, this literally translates to "Holy Blood." The implication was, of course, that the blood of Christ flowed through the Merovingian lineage and thus in the veins of Pierre Plantard.

GET A CLUE!

In April 2006, Justice Peter Smith, the judge in *The Da Vinci Code* plagiarism trial, embedded his own secret code in the seventy-one-page trial ruling, sparking a worldwide race to see who could crack the code first. Reportedly, legal analyst Dan Tench, who first discovered the code, cracked it after receiving a series of e-mail hints from the judge. «

THE SECRET PRIORY

When the Merovingian dynasty eventually fell and its descendants went underground, Plantard said, the Priory of Sion protected them. Other protectors included the Knights Templar and the Freemasons, two groups that, among others, were intimately involved with the Priory in its earlier existence.

Gerard de Sède published a book in 1967 based on Plantard's story. It later intrigued three British journalists, Michael Baigent, Richard Leigh, and Henry Lincoln, who went on a decade-long research quest before writing *Holy Blood, Holy Grail*. These authors later sued Dan Brown for plagiarism after he published *The Da Vinci Code*—which told essentially the same story in fiction as their book had done in nonfiction—and lost.

THE TRUTH *IS* OUT THERE

Whether or not Plantard's story is true—and if he and his cohorts did or didn't create the documents of *Les Dossiers Secrets*—is an ongoing debate. As for Plantard's Masonic connections, an additional theory links Plantard and *Les Dossiers Secrets* to the Swiss Grand Loge Alpina. It is alleged that "Les descendants Merovingiens ou l'enigme du Razes Wisigoth," the first of the four documents, was published at the Swiss lodge. To date there is no proof of this claim, and the lodge itself has denied any involvement.

A "NOON BLUE" APPLE A DAY

The phrase "noon blue apples" refers to an effect in the church at Rennes-le-Château in France. At noon every January 17, sunlight shines through the stained glass to make blue orbs float around a painting of Mary Magdalene kneeling before a skull. Conspiracists say this shows Christ wasn't buried in the Holy Land but in France, at Rennes-le-Château.

One theory suggests Plantard and his colleagues Gerard de Sède and Philippe de Chérisey eventually had a falling out and that Plantard made it known that two of Sède's published parchments were indeed fabricated by Chérisey. There are no firm answers to the mystery of the Priory of Sion, but many exceptional books have been written about the legendary organization's existence and possible connection to the Knights Templar, Freemasons, and other individuals, groups, and events in history.

There's yet another element in all these theories that helps link them together and connect them to America. Behind the conspiracy to hide the bloodline of Jesus, some say, are not only the Masons but another equally well-known group: the Knights of the Temple of St. John—the Templars.

MORE DOSSIER SECRETS

Jeova Sanctus Unus is the pseudonym that Isaac Newton used. Newton was an alchemist, a member of the Royal Society of London, and a Rosicrucian who signed documents he wanted to keep secretive with the pseudonym. According to Dan Brown in *The Lost Symbol*, Newton understood that he was divine, and the sixteen letters in Jeova Sanctus Unus could be rearranged to spell his name in Latin: *Isaacus Neutonuus*.

The Knights Templar: America the Holy Grail

Images of the Knights Templar often lead to thoughts of legendary wars and the brave men who, atop their massive steeds, looked larger than life. Of course, imagination, aided by books and film, has a way of making all things historical appear glamorous while minimizing the realistic struggle and brutality of men in battle. These knights did indeed exist, and while their legend can easily be romanticized, their purpose was far more focused. While the Knights were known for their ferocity in battle, especially during the Crusades, they were equally renowned for their banking skills and business acumen.

WHEN IS A GRAIL NOT A GRAIL?

Despite all the controversy over it, there's not much agreement between researchers over what the Holy Grail actually *is*. As mentioned earlier, some say it's the cup that caught the dying Jesus' blood. Others claim it's a bowl or wide dish. Still others say that it is a stone, possibly the long-sought Philosopher's Stone.

WHERE IS THE GRAIL?

The Knights Templar are associated with one of the greatest of historical mysteries: the locale of the Holy Grail. The Knights Templar have been deeply entrenched in that mystery, with many theories surrounding them as alleged protectors of the Grail and its possible location beneath the Rosslyn Chapel in Scotland.

— GET A CLUE! —

The Grail is one of many Christian symbols that may have pagan roots. Chief among these, of course, is the cross.

Created centuries before Christianity, the *Celtic cross* unites the circle and the cross, or the female circle with the male cross to signify fertility. Many Christians would later identify it with the union of heaven and earth.

Symbolic of Saint Peter's request to be crucified upside down (rather than the way Christ was crucified), the *inverted cross* represents humility or the roots of heaven reaching down to earth.

The *ankh* is an ancient Egyptian symbol that bears similar meaning to the Celtic cross, but it also represents the ability to unlock the mysteries of heaven and earth. Others interpret the union of the T cross of Osiris with the oval of Isis as a symbol of immortality. «

The Knights Templar were warrior monks, a military and religious order of men founded in 1118 by French knight Hughes de Payens. From their inception until they were almost entirely wiped out in 1307, the Templars served as protectors of pilgrims traveling from Europe to the Kingdom of Jerusalem. Taking their name from their headquarters next to the legendary Temple of Solomon, the "Poor Knights of Christ and the

Temple of Solomon" were a monastic order that enjoyed enormous wealth and power.

Though their history is spread across two centuries, the Knights Templar are perhaps best known for their participation in the Crusades, for arguably creating the first formal banking system, and for the mystery surrounding their involvement with the Holy Grail and the Ark of the Covenant. To understand their rise to power and fall from grace, and their possible connection to Freemasons, it's important to examine the role they played in the Crusades from the eleventh to the thirteenth centuries.

THE KNIGHTS TEMPLAR AND MITHRAISM

Echoes of the rites associated with Mithraism appear in the traditions of the Knights Templar, and, in turn, in those of the Freemasons. This is not very surprising, since it is conceivable that in their travels on the Crusade to the Middle East, they would have become familiar with Mithraic folk rituals still practiced there and brought these practices home.

A CRUSADE FOR KNIGHTS

The Crusades were a series of military campaigns sanctioned by the Catholic Church to recover the Holy Land and Jerusalem from the hands of the Muslims. These expeditions took place from 1096 to 1291, with each Crusade focusing on a different goal. The crusades originated with a speech by Pope Urban II, delivered at a church council in Clermont in 1095. At that time, the spread of Islam was proving to be a threat to the Byzantine Empire, and accounts of Christian mistreatment at the hands of Muslims were reaching the West.

The response to Pope Urban's request that the Holy City of Jerusalem be liberated from the infidels was overwhelming. Crusaders quickly showed their commitment by sewing red crosses to their clothing. The true motivation for the pope's decision to incite the Crusades is unknown, but speculation points to a combination of religious reasons and a desire to unite warring factions within Europe.

After successfully taking the Holy City in 1099, Godfrey de Bouillon became the first ruler of the newly created Kingdom of Jerusalem. In 1100, the rule was passed to de Bouillon's brother Baldwin I, who proclaimed himself the first king of Jerusalem. When he passed away, the crown fell to his cousin Baldwin II. In 1118, nine knights approached Baldwin II seeking approval to found a new order whose mission it would be to protect individuals during their pilgrimage to the Holy Land. It was then that the Order of the Knights Templar was born, a strict order of men who took a vow of poverty, chastity, and obedience. Any individual who joined the Knights Templar had to adhere to stringent rules. In addition to taking vows, they slept on straw mattresses, were forbidden to cut their beards, and were only allowed to consume meat three times each week.

THE TEMPLARS ARE FOUNDED

In 1128 at the Council of Troyes, the Knights Templar were given sanction by the church with the assistance of St. Bernard of Clairvaux, who helped establish the rules of the Order. Fifty years later, more than 300 knights proudly wore the traditional white mantle that denoted a Templar. The combined wealth of the order was amassed as a result of donations of both property and monetary funds given over to the Order when wealthy members took their vows of poverty.

By 1135, the Knights began lending money to those making the Holy Land pilgrimage. Money that was kept in temples along the route was well guarded, and travelers could safely deposit funds in exchange for written receipts and then retrieve those funds at another temple farther along the route. In essence, the knights had begun a rudimentary banking system. This system, in addition to making the knights rich, gave the monastic orders a significant boost of power. By 1239, the Templars owned 9,000 castles and manors and were richer than any other continental government. In addition, their numbers had grown to more than 15,000.

Groups possessing such wealth and perceived power, as history can attest, often become the target of those who wish to usurp and attain control of that power. The Knights Templar were victims of such persecution at the hands of their very creators, the church and crown.

French King Philip IV, also known as Philip the Fair, proved to be the undoing of the Knights Templar. A royal who lavishly squandered funds, Philip found himself in serious conflict with the Catholic Church in 1296, when he began taxing the church's holdings to replenish his own coffers. When Pope Boniface VIII threatened to excommunicate the French people, King Philip ordered him kidnapped, only to have the pontiff expire after a short captivity.

It is said that the unscrupulous king then applied to become a Knight Templar and was summarily refused entrance into the Order. He subsequently set about manipulating the election of the next pope, Clement V, who then moved the papacy from Italy to France. Clement and Philip emerged from the affair with an implacable hatred for the Templars.

It is unknown why these two men set out to destroy the Knights Templar. They may have been motivated by envy of the Knights' wealth and power. As well, the king may have wanted to escape his debts to the Order. Whatever the reason, the fall of the Knights Templar started with a summons issued to Templar Grand Master Jacques de Molay

FRIDAY THE THIRTEENTH: THE UNLUCKIEST DAY

Twenty-one-year-old Jacques de Molay had become a Templar in 1265. An ambitious Frenchman, he moved up the ranks and eventually became Grand Master of the Order. Having replaced the Order's previous Grand Master, Theobald Gaudin, de Molay took up residence at the Templar headquarters in Cyprus. In 1307, de Molay received word that he was to return to France on order of King Philip and Pope Clement. He presumed the reason for the summons was to consider another crusade.

De Molay returned to France unaware of the horrible fate that would soon befall him and his fellow Templars. On what would prove an ironic date, October 13, 1307, Knights Templar all over France were arrested. They were tortured, forced to either confess to their alleged misconduct (including Christian heresy, idol worship, sexual perversions, and satanic worship); or face death.

THE ORDER OF DE MOLAY IN AMERICA

In 1919 in Kansas City, Missouri, a businessman named Frank S. Land founded an American Masonic fraternal organization for boys ages twelve to twenty-one. Named for Grand Master Jacques de Molay, its alumni now include such well-known Americans as Bill Clinton, Walt Disney, and Pete Rose.

Under extreme duress, de Molay offered a confession that he would later recant. As a result, he and a fellow Templar were burned alive in 1312 in Paris within view of Notre Dame.

Many legends revolve around the Knights Templar, and one is that just before de Molay died, he issued a prophecy that both King Philip and Pope Clement would die within a year's time. As it turned out, both men did die within the following year. However, the pope, just prior to his death, dealt a fatal blow to the Templars with a final order stating that any individual who joined the Order would be excommunicated from the church as a heretic. In fact, it is said that the modern-day superstition about Friday the Thirteenth derives from the fateful day in 1307 when the Knights Templar were arrested and summarily tortured and killed.

THE TEMPLARS IN SCOTLAND

There is no consensus about what became of the Templars after their persecution by King Philip IV. Many believe that a number of Templars who escaped arrest and execution made their way to Scotland in search of a safe haven. Since Scotland's king, Robert Bruce, had already been excommunicated from the Church, it stands to reason that the Templars would join with the Scots, who were in great need of assistance in their battles against the English for independence.

It is said that after a successful battle against the English foe, the Templars were given refuge on a Scottish isle, where they remained for the next eighty years. Certain theorists and historians contend that these rogue Templars eventually became a more permanent brotherhood known as . . . Freemasons.

The Knights Templar have been a subject of both scholarly research and popular fiction for centuries. Legends of their hidden treasures, secret rituals, and political power have figured over the years in medieval romances and Victorian novels. In recent decades, they have moved into the spotlight with modern bestsellers such as *The Da Vinci Code* and action films like *Indiana Jones and the Last Crusade* and *National Treasure.*

The Knights have also been portrayed as guardians of the legendary Holy Grail.

A CHURCH BUILT OF CLUES

Another legend suggests that when the Knight Templars were outlawed by the Catholic Church and fled to Scotland, taking their secrets and their treasures with them, some settled around the small town of Rosslyn, where they gave their secrets to the Freemasons. The Freemasons in turn built the famous Rosslyn Chapel, supposedly along the same architectural lines as the Temple of Solomon. Filled with fabulous and mystifying symbolism, this church was created on the orders of William Sinclair, believed to be one of the secret leaders of the Priory of Sion.

The symbols in the church may contain musical notes that together form a clue to the location of the treasure. Perhaps they are coordinates for a buried vault. Some of the symbols seem to suggest ears of corn and the leaves of the aloe plant, despite the fact that neither were known in Europe at the time and both originated in North America.

But why secret symbols in a church? Why not just put the information in a book and lock it in a vault? Well, because the conspirators were Freemasons, and that's what masons do—they build things.

The Knights Templar, American Style

You'll find evidence of the influence of the Knights of the Templar all around us:

- *Indiana Jones and the Last Crusade*
- Friday the Thirteenth
- The Order of De Molay

- The York Rite, a collection of Masonic degrees in the United States, whose final order is known as the Knights Templar
- *Assassin's Creed* and *Dragon Age*, popular video games
- The Federal Triangle in Washington, D.C. Some researchers have suggested that this triangle mimics one found at Rennes-le-Chateau and associated with the Templars.

The Knights Templar and the Scottish Rite: Saved by an American

"In his interpretation of Masonic symbolism, Albert Pike naturally turned, as scholars must ultimately do, to those ancient institutions of learning from which has descended to this age the whole bounty of rationale good."

—Manly Palmer Hall

The connection between the Knights Templar and Freemasons is a subject that is still vehemently debated. Many feel that the Templars who ended up in Scotland gave birth to the Scottish Rite, one of the two major branches of Freemasonry. Other historians argue that the Masons simply adopted the romantic and chivalrous history of the Knights Templar, one that would provide infinitely more backbone and drama to their history.

Given the climate of the era, one can also theorize that a persecuted order, such as the Templars, would naturally gravitate toward a secret fraternal organization in its infancy. Whatever the case may be, there is no definitive proof of a Masonic connection to the Knights Templar of legend, but there are plenty of facts and myths that make the Order a very attractive relative. To determine how this might be the case, we need to understand something of the way in which American Freemasons are organized.

THE AMERICAN BRANCHES

Once an individual has passed through the three main degrees, or levels, of Freemasonry—Entered Apprentice, Fellowcraft, and Master Mason—he can continue his education with other branches of Freemasonry.

The Brotherhood consists of two main branches, one of which is the York Rite, and the other the Ancient and Accepted Scottish Rite, or Scottish Rite as it is commonly called. In the York rite, the final order is known as the Knights Templar. Masons belong to one or another of the two branches.

The Scottish Rite consists of thirty-three degrees, each serving to extend a Mason's knowledge of the Craft. An individual wishing to become a thirty-third degree Mason of the Scottish Rite cannot apply for the degree. Masons who show exemplary community leadership and who exemplify the principles of the Brotherhood must be elected by a unanimous vote.

THE LOST MASON

In Dan Brown's *The Lost Symbol*, Robert Langdon's friend Peter Solomon, whose disappearance sets in motion the events of the novel, is a thirty-third degree Mason.

The origin of the Scottish Rite appears to be lost in antiquity, but one school of thought suggests its roots are with the Knights Templar who lived in exile in Scotland after their Order was banished. Others say that the rite originated with expatriate Scotsmen, who created a lodge in France. Records show that it wasn't until 1804 that the name *Ancient and Accepted Scottish Rite* appeared in documents between the Grand Orient of France and the Supreme Council of France. In the United States, the Scottish Rite is divided into Northern and Southern Jurisdictions that are governed by Supreme Councils.

ALBERT PIKE REVIVES THE KNIGHTS TEMPLAR LEGACY

In the nineteenth century, Freemasonry suffered a decline in the United States. To revive it, a former Confederate military officer named Albert Pike wrote *Morals and Dogma,* a massive book on the Scottish Rite, published in 1871. This work renewed Masonry's popularity once again (though, ironically, few actually read it) and presented Freemasonry as the true repository of the esoteric secrets and arcane knowledge that make up the Ancient Mysteries.

> *"Masonry is identical with the Ancient Mysteries."*
>
> —Albert Pike

MORALS AND DOGMA MEETS THE LOST SYMBOL

In *Morals and Dogma,* Pike maintained that the degrees earned in the Scottish Rite were steeped in the Ancient Mysteries of Egypt, Asia, and Greece. These Ancient Mysteries also provide the themes of Dan Brown's *The Lost Symbol.* In this bestselling thriller, Brown's protagonist, Robert Langdon, comes face to face with a bronze bust of "Masonic luminary" Albert Pike in the Masonic House of the Temple in Washington, D.C.

Pike was not universally liked, and his actions in fighting against the Union were held against him by some. His dense prose style warded off readers, and he seems to have been both arrogant and difficult. Nonetheless, he is a significant figure in the post–Civil War revival of Freemasonry in the United States.

Do You Know the Way to San Jose and the Rosicrucians?

Besides the Templars, another connection to the Masons and to the Ancient Mysteries comes from the strange order of the Rosicrucians.

A ROSE IS A ROSE

Many believe the name Rosicrucian evolved from the Latin words for dew (*ros*) and cross (*crux*). They claim that the dew represents the alchemical dew of the philosophers, which equated to the most powerful solvent of gold. The cross represents the coming together or enlightenment of its members. According to modern Rosicrucians, the rosy cross predated Christianity and symbolically represents the human body, and the rose represents the individual's unfolding consciousness.

The Rosicrucians were a secret society that emerged in Europe in the early 1600s. Their aim was no less than the moral renewal and perfection of mankind. Their mystical philosophy appears to have been greatly influenced by the Ancient Mysteries, as well as the march of modern science. The band of brothers espoused the philosophy that all educated men throughout the world should establish a synthesis of science, through which a perfect method for all the arts would emerge.

The American branch of the Rosicrucian order of the Ancient and Mystical Order of the Rosy Cross (AMORC), with headquarters in San Jose, California, traces its brother/sisterhood philosophy to the "heretical" Egyptian pharaoh Akhenaten, who founded monotheism. Other Rosicrucian societies trace their founding to Christian Rosenkreutz, who appears in one of the key Rosicrucian texts that helped define Rosicrucian philosophy: *Fama Fraternitatis* (published in 1614). Rosenkreutz supposedly learned the science of alchemy in the East. Many also believe that Rosenkreutz (literally "rose cross" in German) was a pseudonym used by Francis Bacon.

THOMAS JEFFERSON'S SECRET ROSICRUCIAN CODES

Thomas Jefferson was not only our third president, but also a scientist, architect, and diplomat whose love for ciphers served him well in all of these areas. Known as the American Cryptographer, Jefferson even created a wheel cipher so ingenious that people still use it more than 200 years later. According to Dr. H. Spencer Lewis of the AMORC, Jefferson also used a code found in "ancient Rosicrucian secret manuscripts"; evidence of this code was found among Jefferson's papers.

THE ANCIENT MYSTERIES OF EGYPT

The Rosicrucian movement has its roots in the mystery traditions, philosophy, and myths of ancient Egypt dating back to approximately 1500 BCE. Rosicrucian tradition relates that the great pyramids of Giza were sacred in the eyes of initiates. Contrary to what historians affirm, Rosicrucians believe that the Giza pyramids were constructed to serve as sacred places for the study and mystical initiation into the Ancient Mysteries—and not as tombs of pharaohs.

GET A CLUE!

The Rosicrucian symbol honors the blood of Christ that stained the cross, by pairing the arms of the cross with roses. Some rosy crosses will have one rose in the center, with seven petals to represent the seven stages of initiation or regeneration. Other rosy crosses will have four roses in each corner of the cross to represent the unfolding of spiritual realities within.

The rose cross is a common symbol in Freemasonry. One of the degrees of the Scottish Rites is called the "Knights of the Rose Cross," which honors their ancestors, the early Rosicrucians. «

THE ALCHEMY OF ROSICRUCIANISM

Alchemy—the art of transmutation—came into prominence with the Alexandrian Greeks. It was then introduced to the Arabs, who then transmitted it to Europe. Alchemists played a tremendous part in the early history of the Rosicrucian Order. While many alchemists were interested in making gold, some were more concerned with the transmutation of human character.

European alchemists and Knights Templar, in contact with the Arab civilization at the time of the Crusades, brought much of this wisdom to the West. In Europe the transcendental alchemists—mystics and philosophers—sought to transmute the base elements of human character into the more noble virtues and to recognize and to unleash the wisdom of the divine self within the individual. Some of the renowned alchemists who were also Rosicrucians or were closely associated with them include:

- Albertus Magnus (1193–1280)
- Roger Bacon (1214–1294)
- Paracelsus (1493–1541)
- Cagliostro (1743–1795)
- Nicolas Flamel (1330–1418)
- Robert Fludd (1574–1637)

Unfortunately, over the next few centuries, tyrannical rulers or those bound to narrow religious systems persecuted the alchemists for transmitting the ancient knowledge. During these times, the Rosicrucians went underground, yet they never ceased their activities, perpetuating their ideals and their teachings. They put the advancement of the arts, sciences, and civilization above their own safety, and they truly believed in the equality of men and women and the true solidarity of all humanity.

GET A CLUE!

The rose was considered an alchemical symbol for perfection. In Christianity, the red rose symbolizes the Virgin Mother or the blood shed by Jesus on the cross. A rose often implies secrecy. Three roses are a potent Masonic symbol, representing light, love, and life. «

As the Renaissance burst upon Europe the *Fama Fraternitatis*, first published in seventeenth-century Germany, heralded a renewed interest in Rosicrucianism throughout Europe. The *Fama* introduces Christian Rosenkreutz, a character who travels to centers of learning in the Near East and who personifies the revived interest in esoteric studies and mystical learning. During this time, Sir Francis Bacon (1561–1626), an English philosopher, essayist, and statesman, directed the Rosicrucian Order and its activities both in England and on the continent, and many believe that he used the name Christian Rosenkreutz as a pseudonym.

ROSICRUCIANS IN AMERICA

In the late seventeenth century, following a plan originally proposed by Sir Francis Bacon in *The New Atlantis*, a colony of Rosicrucian leaders was organized to establish the Rosicrucian arts and sciences in America. In 1694 Rosicrucian settlers made the perilous journey across the Atlantic Ocean in a specially chartered vessel and established their first settlement in Philadelphia, later moving further west in Pennsylvania to Ephrata. The Rosicrucians soon made valuable contributions to the newly emerging American culture, most particularly in the fields of printing, philosophy, the sciences, and the arts.

THE MYSTIC ORDER IN PENNSYLVANIA

Ephrata, Pennsylvania, was also the seat of The Mystic Order of the Solitary, a group of monastic Seventh-Day Dunkers. Members of the order practiced celibacy and vegetarianism and devoted their lives to prayer and hard work.

Among the Founding Fathers, Benjamin Franklin, Thomas Jefferson, and Thomas Paine were intimately connected with the Rosicrucian community.

Throughout history, there have been periods of greater and lesser activity of Rosicrucianism around the world. When curiosity and interest in the Order faded in the Americas during the nineteenth century, it remained very active in France, Germany, Switzerland, Russia, and Spain, among others.

In 1909 the American businessman and philosopher H. Spencer Lewis journeyed to France, where he was duly initiated into the Rosicrucian Order and chartered with the responsibility of renewing Rosicrucian activity in America. With Lewis as its president, the Rosicrucian Order, AMORC, was incorporated in 1915 in New York City, thereafter moving to San Francisco and, for a time, Tampa, Florida. In 1927 the Order moved its headquarters to San Jose, California, where it remains today.

PHILADELPHIA, ROSICRUCIAN CITY OF BROTHERLY LOVE

The City of Brotherly Love was the first home of the Rosicrucians in America. The rose—which is an anagram of the Greek word *eros*, or love—was one of their major symbols, representing their belief in the concept of brotherly love. While Philadelphia comes from the Greek words *philos* for friendship and *adelphos* for brother, it seems an ironic synchronicity that the proponents of brotherly love first landed in the New World in the City of Brotherly Love.

Throughout history a number of prominent persons in the fields of science and the arts have been associated with the Rosicrucian movement, including:

- Leonardo da Vinci (1452–1519)
- Cornelius Heinrich Agrippa (1486–1535)
- Paracelsus (1493–1541)
- François Rabelais (1494–1553)
- Theresa of Avila (1515–1582)
- John of the Cross (1542–1591)
- Francis Bacon (1561–1626)
- Robert Fludd (1574–1637)
- Jacob Boehme (1575–1624)
- René Descartes (1596–1650)
- Blaise Pascal (1623–1662)
- Baruch Spinoza (1632–1677)

- Isaac Newton (1642–1727)
- Gottfried Wilhelm Leibniz (1646–1716)
- Benjamin Franklin (1706–1790)
- Thomas Jefferson (1743–1826)
- Michael Faraday (1791–1867)
- Ella Wheeler Wilcox (1850–1919)
- Marie Corelli (1855–1924)
- Claude Debussy (1862–1918)
- Erik Satie (1866–1925)
- Edith Piaf (1916–1963)

THE ROSE OF THE SEXES

Rosicrucianism is the only "secret" society that invited women to play an equal role, without regard to religion or race.

Similar to Freemasonry, applicants to the Rosicrucian Order had to be considered "worthy," which meant they had to display a fervent interest or deep desire to immerse themselves in knowledge in the mysteries and meet certain criteria, or tests. Over the course of centuries, Rosicrucian societies added an initiatory dimension to the knowledge they transmitted.

Conclusion: All Roads Lead to Freemasons

As we've seen in Part One, much of our secret heritage ultimately leads to the Freemasons. Whether you're discussing ancient philosophers or our founding fathers, the greatest minds of the Renaissance or the most prominent citizens in twenty-first-century America, the Freemasons are bound to come up sooner or later.

In Part Two, we'll explore the fascinating origins of this one-of-a-kind secret and not-so-secret society.

FREEMASONRY: THE GREAT REPOSITORY OF AMERICAN SECRETS

Freemasonry is the oldest and largest fraternal organization in the world. It is a social and educational group well known for its philanthropic work with numerous charities. Often called a "secret society," the fraternity, arguably more misunderstood than elusive, has attracted and nurtured thousands of individuals and communities over the centuries. Despite all the speculation and conspiracies surrounding the Brotherhood, or perhaps because of them, the bond between Freemasons has endured and flourished.

And nowhere have the Freemasons endured and flourished more than in the United States of America—a nation founded and built on Masonic principles steeped in its traditions. In Part Two, we'll learn how the Freemasons survived all threats to their existence, and why they set their sights on the New World— where they took root and flourished. Most important, we'll discover how this esoteric organization continues to influence our nation today.

CHAPTER 4

FREEMASONS: THE LIGHT BEARERS OF THE ANCIENT MYSTERIES

At face value, Freemasons are a benevolent, social, charitable organization whose members seek to learn more about themselves in order to benefit their families and communities. But dig deeper, and you find that Masons are knowledge seekers, their fraternal education focusing on lessons that help them on a journey to achieve moral and spiritual enlightenment. This enlightenment comes from the Ancient Mysteries—and thanks to will, determination, and the sacrifice of the Freemasons throughout history, the Ancient Mysteries live on, for those willing to uncover their hidden truths.

CRAFT OR CULT?

Freemasonry is often referred to as Masonry, the Brotherhood, or the Craft. The members are called brothers, and the membership within a lodge is referred to as brethren.

They are nonsectarian, and while their membership must profess a belief in a Supreme Being, it can be any deity. Individuals of all faiths are welcome to join.

So what's all the hoopla about? Why is so little known about such an historic organization? Why so much controversy? In truth, there is plenty of information on Freemasonry both in print and on the web, but more often than not it's a bit confusing and often limited to a specific opinion or theory. At the root of the problem is, perhaps, their alleged secrecy, but in reality all Masons are free to acknowledge their membership, and their rules, constitutions, rituals, and ceremonies have all been written about publicly.

Despite the mythology surrounding Freemasonry, it's not a religion or a religious cult. Its members are not Satanists or Luciferians. Its rituals are not bloody oaths to the death. They're not a political organization, and above all, they're not a secret group of powerful men hell bent on achieving world domination.

Who Are the Masons, Really?

Despite the astounding amount of information available on the Brotherhood—including literature, historical records, documentaries, archives, websites, legends, expert commentary, anti-Masonic conjecture, and conspiratorial speculation—there remain many diverse opinions in regard to who they really are, what they do, and how they evolved.

FROM SOLOMON TO THE NEW WORLD

Historians, scholars, writers, and researchers have dedicated an impressive amount of ink and energy in attempting to discover the true origin of Freemasonry. It's a subject that to this day remains a constant source of debate. One theory goes back as far as the construction of King Solomon's Temple in Jerusalem during the eighth century BC. One of the legends that permeates Masonic rituals and teachings revolves around King Solomon's Master Mason, Hiram Abiff. His story and tragic death play a great role in Freemasonry.

THE STORY OF HIRAM ABIFF

There are many competing interpretations of the legend of Hiram Abiff. However, the basic story is as follows:

When Solomon was building his temple, he sent to the King of Tyre for assistance. The king sent Solomon his most talented architect, Hiram Abiff, a widow's son. As mentioned earlier, Solomon became jealous of Hiram, either because the architect had become the lover of Solomon's wife or for other unspecified reasons. (Other legends absolve Solomon of any responsibility for Hiram's death.)

Whatever the case, Solomon arranged for three ruffians to attack Hiram: Jubela, Jubelo, and Jubelum, known collectively as the three Juwes. The three confronted Hiram and demanded that he tell them the Secret Name of God.

When the architect refused, Jubela struck Hiram in the throat with a gauge, Jubelo hit him in the chest with an architect's square, and Jubelum attacked him with a gavel. They removed the body from the city and buried it outside Jerusalem's walls.

According to some accounts, Solomon, perhaps repentant for his deed, raised Hiram from the dead, using the third degree Mason's grip and whispering in the architect's ear the syllables "Ma-Ha-Bone." The three Juwes were captured and executed for the murder.

As we indicated in Part One, many individuals have speculated that Freemasons are somehow linked to the valiant Knights Templar. Though no proven links have been established, there has been much written about the Masons and their possible connection to the Templars, and by association to such legendary artifacts as the Holy Grail and the Ark of the Covenant.

Another school of thought is that Freemasons evolved from Medieval Masonic Guilds, but the generally accepted beginning of organized Masonry is the formation of the Grand Lodge of England in 1717.

Prior to the formation of organized Freemasonry, stonemasons of the Medieval Age were making their mark all over Europe, and the splendor and artistry of their work is highly revered by modern art historians. The formation of the Freemasons was, to some extent, a reflection of the high esteem in which masons were held. As the Middle Ages drew to a close, the order endured setbacks as a result of the Protestant Reformation. But like a phoenix, it was resurrected to new heights and notoriety to form what is now a Brotherhood of legend.

As we discussed earlier, Freemasonry is divided into the Scottish Rite and the York Rite. We've talked a bit about the Scottish Rite in Part One, and we'll come back to it later. For now, let's examine the York Rite.

THE YORK RITE

The York Rite, which derives its name from the city of York in the North of England, constitutes the second concordant body of Freemasonry. There are three bodies within the York Rite, including Royal Arch Masonry, Cryptic Masonry, and Knights Templar. These groups confer additional degrees for Masons interested in further enlightenment and study of the Brotherhood.

The origin of the York Rite has been a fascinating source of study and debate for historians, scholars, and Freemasons themselves. Degrees conferred upon Masons through the York Rite and its associated bodies are understandably steeped in history and lore and represent a great source of pride throughout the Brotherhood.

Is Masonry a Religion?

One of the biggest misconceptions about Freemasonry is that it is a religion. It must be said that Freemasons do not claim to be a religion or some type of religious substitute. That doesn't mean its members aren't religious, because all of the brethren are required to profess a belief in a Supreme Being. This simply means they aren't an institutionalized system of worship. They're a fraternity that encourages its brethren to be active in whichever religion and church they profess.

For those unfamiliar with Freemasonry, the religious aspects of the Craft can certainly be confusing. Writings about the Brotherhood often mention a bible, Masons meet in temples, many of their symbols have historically religious connotations, and some of their titles contain words like *worshipful* and *priest*. It's easy to see why misunderstandings occur. But in this case, a Worshipful Master has nothing to do with actual worship as a religious reference. It is, in fact, a title of honor, much like one would address the mayor of a city.

There are several basic elements to consider when analyzing Freemasonry in regard to religion. For starters, the organization has no dogma or central theology, and members are free to practice any religion to which they subscribe. Unlike most organized religions, the Masons have no sacramental offerings or ritual worship, and the Brotherhood does not offer salvation in the traditional religious sense of the word. All Masonic titles are purely symbolic and honorable.

SACRED TEXTS OF THE FREEMASONS

Freemasons don't have a Masonic bible. They have a Volume of the Sacred Law, which is present and open at every Masonic gathering. During initiation ceremonies, a candidate can have on the altar or table whichever sacred text he wishes.

Masons are often referred to as "operative" or "speculative." Operative Masons are those Freemasons who are actually, well, masons. That is, they practice the trade of masonry. Speculative

Masons, the overwhelming majority of Freemasons, are not directly connected to the trade of masonry.

When speculative Freemasonry originated in the eighteenth century, most of its members were Christian. As such, the Holy Bible, particularly the King James version, was the Volume of Sacred Law used in most lodges. Freemasons, however, are tolerant of all religions. In lodges with memberships comprising a variety of faiths, several different sacred texts, such as the Koran or Torah, may be used.

A curious criticism, among others, in regard to the Masonic use of the Bible as a volume of Sacred Law is their reference to it as "furniture." This classification, which sounds odd to non-Masons (especially when taken out of context) is not meant to be disrespectful. The use of the word *furniture* is inclusive to Masons as it stands for "essential equipment" during lodge meetings. The sacred text is given a place of honor in a lodge, and it lies open on an altar, table, or pedestal.

Grand Architect of the Universe

One of the basic qualifications an individual must possess when applying to become a Freemason is the belief in a Supreme Being and the immortality of the soul. The Brotherhood doesn't interfere with any member's religion, but asks that all members hold their own faith in a Supreme Being in high regard.

The letter G, which is commonly used in Masonic symbolism with a square and compass, alternately stands for geometry, God, or the Masonic preference, Grand Architect of the Universe. The latter addresses deity in a nonsectarian manner, which gives brothers the ability to focus on their own Supreme Being. Differences in religion between the brethren don't really play a part in the fraternity, because religion and politics are not allowed to be discussed in a lodge.

THE SEARCH FOR DIVINE TRUTH AND LIGHT

Religion definitely plays a part in Freemasonry, but the organization strongly believes in religious freedom, which is why membership is open to individuals of any religion. It also believes that a person's relationship to deity is both sacred and private.

A Mason's search for Divine Truth and Light is often misunderstood as being a search for salvation. That is not the case. Masonic references to "light" refer to knowledge. Masons are in a search for knowledge, which includes educational and spiritual enlightenment, and not salvation. In a similar vein, Masonry professes a hope in the concept of resurrection, unlike a religion that promises resurrection. Freemasons believe that a path to man's salvation is found not in their lodge, but in their chosen house of worship.

Deism and Freemasonry

Another intriguing connection with Masonry is the thinkers who call their religious views Deist. Deism and Freemasonry have an interesting history. Author J. G. Findel, who wrote *History of Freemasonry* in 1865, offered intriguing speculation about the relationship between Deists and Masons.

WHAT IS DEISM?

Deists believe that the universe was created by a supreme being (though they do not always call it "God"). However, they don't believe that this being imposes Himself into the lives of human beings. His nature can be deduced, they suggest, from the natural laws he set in motion. In this view, God started the world going and then stepped back and let it alone. Deists reject organized religion, and they focus on reasoning as the key element to all knowledge. Deism is sometimes called *natural religion* or *the religion of nature*.

Deists of the seventeenth and eighteenth centuries included many freethinkers, including:

- Thomas Jefferson (1743–1826)
- Benjamin Franklin (1706–1790)
- Voltaire (1694–1778)
- René Descartes (1596–1650)
- Lord Herbert of Cherbury (1583–1648)

In his book, Findel asserted that these great thinkers had significant influence on Freemasonry and that they contributed to its transformation from an "Operative to a universal Speculative Society." Findel's speculation was certainly cause for Masonic debate. It is said that in Anderson's *Constitutions*, the term "irreligious Libertine" refers to the Deists of the time, which suggests they had little to do with the fraternal organization.

During this period, Masonic thought in the United States was dominated by Christianity. That has all changed with the modern era, and Freemasonry would not reject a member who is a Deist. When a man decides to join the Brotherhood and becomes an initiate, none of the brethren is allowed to question him as to his religious or political affiliations. Every Mason brings his own beliefs to the Craft.

GNOSTICISM AND FREEMASONS

Built on doctrines of Jewish, pre-Christian, and early Christian sects that focused on the knowledge of God and the beginning and end of humankind, Gnosticism was considered heretical by the Roman Catholic Church. Once thought lost to antiquity, several important texts known collectively as the Gnostic Gospels have surfaced over the past century, including the Gospels of Thomas, Philip, Mary, Mary Magdalene, and even Judas. These discoveries have renewed interest in Gnosticism, which many believe also lived on in the Masonic tradition.

Apprentice to the Light

The Entered Apprentice is the first degree of Freemasonry. In many ways it symbolizes an individual's spiritual birth into the fraternity, and it begins his quest for "light," or knowledge. It is a preliminary degree, which serves to prepare the individual for the second and third degrees. Those will, in succession, elevate his level of fraternal education, understanding, and enlightenment.

GET A CLUE!

In Dan Brown's *The Lost Symbol,* the villain, Mal'akh, has a series of tattoos on his body, all arranged in a meaningful order. His feet have tattoos of the talons of a hawk; his legs have tattoos of Solomon's Temple columns, called Boaz and Joachim; his pelvis has a tattoo of an arch; his chest has a tattoo of a double-headed phoenix. These tattoos are Masonic symbols that represent the ascending order in reaching toward the Godhead. In the novel, the character leaves his crown bare, awaiting the discovery of the final symbol, which he intends to tattoo on his head so he can sacrifice himself and make his transition. «

In order to obtain each degree, a member must participate in a symbolic ritual before he can continue on to the next degree. This begins with the Entered Apprentice degree and the first of an initiate's catechisms, or questions and examinations. Typically, a new member will work with an existing member to aid in the memorization of the questions and answers that relate to that degree. When a catechism is completed, an initiate can move on to his next degree.

Each degree has certain symbolism associated with its level. These symbols, or working tools, are meant to represent the morals and forces necessary in building and rebuilding the nature of humankind. Philosophically, the tools, by their very nature, are meant to show that well-meaning and gratifying work, with proper guidance, can be accomplished. The working tools of the Entered Apprentice degree are the common gavel (a tool of force) and the twenty-four-inch gauge (a tool of calculation and measurement).

As an Apprentice, an individual is introduced to the lodge and the internal structure of the fraternity. The lessons he learns begin with his initiation rite, where he must be prepared to embark on a personal journey of educational and spiritual fulfillment. Once an individual is duly ready to accept this journey, he can proceed to the second degree, or Fellowcraft.

Spiritual Tools of Fellowcraft

Individuals who earn the second degree of Freemasonry, called Fellowcraft, are symbolically entering into the adult phase of the Craft. At this stage, members seek to acquire the knowledge and spiritual tools necessary to build character and improve society. The symbolism associated with the second degree differs from the first in that more science is introduced to the individual. Additional allegories and symbols serve to further enhance the initiate's intellectual prowess and reasoning capabilities.

The Fellowcraft degree symbolizes life and the emergence into spiritual adulthood. In keeping with his progressive fraternal education, the initiate is taught more history of the Craft, and the legacy of operative Masonry from biblical to medieval times. During this symbolic period of manhood, Fellowcraft initiates use the lessons they learned as an Entered Apprentice to broaden and strengthen their horizons.

UP THE WINDING STAIRCASE

The primary symbol associated with a Fellowcraft Mason is a winding staircase, which is used to ascend to new spiritual heights. He is also introduced to pillars and the letter G, which holds special significance for the Brotherhood.

Master Mason of the Craft

Throughout the fraternity, it is a commonly held belief that there is no higher degree conferred on an individual than Master Mason. Degrees earned beyond Master through one of the concordant bodies, such as the York and Scottish Rites, are generally considered to be educational and symbolic.

The Master Mason is symbolically linked to the soul and his own inner nature and belief system. His spiritual and physical growth is enhanced when achieving this degree, as he climbs the winding stairs of adulthood in an effort to learn more of the Divine Truth. The degree is richly laden with allegory and symbolism that dates back to the building of the Temple of Solomon, and the rites associated with the degree are taken very seriously in regard to a brother's spiritual and educational teachings of the Craft.

Once an individual has become a Mason, meaning he has completed the first three degrees and is now a Master Mason, he is free to continue his education by joining the Scottish or York Rite. The Scottish Rite consists of thirty-two degrees and an honorary thirty-third degree, which is by invitation only and is conferred by the Supreme Council.

The York Rite features three additional Masonic bodies—Royal Arch Masonry, Cryptic Masonry, and Knights Templar—

that confer degrees within their ranks. Master Masons also have the option of joining one of Masonry's social groups, such as the Shriners.

SMALL-SCREEN BROTHERHOODS

Television has had its share of fictional fraternities, most presumably drawing influence from real fraternal organizations like the Masons, Shriners, Elks, and others. Many of the classic sitcoms had—for better or for worse—fictional fraternal links. *Dallas* had the Daughters of the Alamo, *Dobie Gillis* had the Benevolent Order of the Bison, and *Northern Exposure* featured the Sons of the Tundra.

On *Mama's Family*, starring Vicki Lawrence, Ken Berry's character (Vinton Harper) joined the Cobra Lodge, which was under the guidance of the Grand Viper. They had a secret hissing cobra handshake, and anyone violating their oaths was hissed out of the lodge.

OTHER SMALL SCREEN FRATERNITIES INCLUDE:

Married with Children. Al Bundy was a member of the misogynist National Organization of Men Against Amazonian Masterhood.

Happy Days. Howard Cunningham was a member of the Leopard Lodge.

The Honeymooners. Ralph Kramden and his best pal, Ed Norton, were members of the Raccoons.

Laverne and Shirley. Lenny and Squiggy were initiated into the Fraternal Order of the Bass.

The Drew Carey Show. Drew's father was a member of the Wildebeests.

Cheers. Cliff Clavin belonged to an alcohol-free lodge called the Knights of the Scimitar.

The Andy Griffith Show. Andy and Barney were members of the Regal Order of the Golden Door to Good Fellowship. The Order's password was "Geronimo!"

Masonic Rituals, Ceremonies, and Initiations

Masonic rites are serious, dignified ceremonies rich in allegory and symbolism. Freemasonry isn't a religion, but its rituals are held in the same regard as one holds ceremonies and rites associated with various churches and religions. Each allegory, symbol, or legend used in Masonic rituals and ceremonies holds great meaning within the Brotherhood. Some symbols, like the apron or a gavel, may seem out of context, but their meaning is highly symbolic to ancient Masonry as the tools of the trade.

When a member is initiated into the Brotherhood, he enters a world filled with ritual, allegory, symbolism, and history. As he progresses through the three main degrees of Freemasonry, his knowledge and enlightenment increase the higher he climbs. Initiation rites require preparation, including the various catechisms individuals must take to heart and memorize.

EXPOSÉ!

Englishman Samuel Prichard was the first non-Mason to expose allegedly secret Masonic rituals to the public. In 1730 he published *Masonry Dissected*. Until that time, Masonic rituals had been memorized and passed on within the Brotherhood by means of oral communication. Ironically, many Masons purchased the book in order to study their own rituals!

A candidate's primary initiation into the Craft is highly significant, and the rite he endures signifies his earnest, heartfelt promise to be taught, learn from those he teaches, and ultimately lead a better life as a result of those teachings. Initiates are encouraged to pay close attention to ceremonial proceedings, as with each degree the allegory and symbolism impart additional history of Freemasonry.

Initiation of the First Degree: Entered Apprentice

The initiation rite of the Entered Apprentice, called the Rite of Destitution, is replete with symbolism and mystery, but it is only an inkling of what is to come during the course of an initiate's Masonic career. For starters, the initiate is "duly and truly" prepared, which means he will wear garments that the lodge provides. This signifies an initiate's sincerity in joining the Brotherhood, as the focus is on his presence as a man and lacks any designation of personal honor and wealth.

One of the principles of Freemasonry is charity. By symbolically stripping a man of his wealth or perceived wealth, an initiate learns what it is to be in dire need. It is said that this ritual opens the initiate's eyes to the obligations one has to help mankind in order to bring him out of his desperate plight and help him regain his dignity.

The Rite of Destitution itself is interesting, as it relates to ancient times and planetary characteristics. In long ago times, it is said, men adhered to a belief that the soul was descended from planetary bodies with innate qualities specific to each sphere. Each of the planetary attributes were associated with a type of metal, and as such, initiates rid themselves of all metals prior to ceremonies so that potentially disturbing planetary influences would not pollute the proceedings. In modern times, the rite instead focuses on the shedding of one's image, in a sense, and leaving any prejudice or extreme view out of the lodge so as to retain fraternal harmony.

HOODS AND ROPES?

Part of the initiation rites for the various degrees involve a hoodwink, which refers to a blindfold or hood, and a cable tow, which is a rope used for restraint or towing. Looking at the ritual from the outside, the use of these items may conjure up images of violence or hanging, but that is certainly not the case. The cable tow, which is also a measure of distance, symbolically binds each Mason to all of his brethren. The tie is as strong and lengthy as the Mason and the personal abilities he brings to the Brotherhood.

Being hoodwinked represents the veil of silence and secrecy surrounding the mysteries of the Brotherhood. It is also meant to symbolize the ignorance or "mystical darkness" of an uninitiated member. The hood symbolically remains in place until the initiate is prepared to encompass the "light," or knowledge that is about to be imparted to him. Being blindfolded or hoodwinked also enables the initiate to completely focus on the ceremonial words being spoken without visual distraction. Taken literally, the terms *hood* (as a verb, to "cover"), and *wink* (an archaic reference to the eye) together mean to cover one's eyes.

The cable tow has several symbolic meanings, one of which is an umbilical cord, a necessary factor in the beginnings of life, which is severed upon birth. The cable tow is also regarded as a symbol of acceptance—complete and voluntary—by the initiate, who in participating in the ceremony of hoodwinking also pledges to comply with whatever the fraternity has planned for him.

ENTERING INTO THE LIGHT

When the initiate is "duly" clothed and hoodwinked, he is led into the lodge by the cable tow. Entering into the room in this manner allows the initiate to symbolically leave the darkness and destitution of the world behind him and find embrace in the warmth of light. Initiation rites are highly confidential and are taken very seriously among members. The structure of this rite is meant to reinforce to the initiate that actions have consequences and that virtue plays a large part in gaining entrance into the fraternity and the mysteries surrounding it.

THE HOLY BIBLE, THE SQUARE, AND THE COMPASS

Integral to the Apprentice initiation rite are the Three Great Lights of Masonry. The Volume of the Sacred Law, the square, and the compass acknowledge man's relationship to deity and are another holy trinity of Freemasonry, similar in interpretation to the three degrees. It is said that each Great Light is a guiding principle of nature, with the square symbolizing the body, the compass representing the mind, and the Sacred Law serving as the soul.

The first of these lights is the Volume of the Sacred Law, and depending on the lodge and the area or country, it can be a number of sacred texts. In the United States, that volume is typically the Bible, but initiates are given the option to have the sacred book of their choosing on the altar during their initiation ceremony. The book is placed on the altar and is open, which is highly significant as it acts as a guide to faith and to acknowledge man's relationship to deity.

The square and the compass are the most recognizable symbols in Freemasonry, and their evolution is apparent in many ancient works. The square signifies earth and the compass symbolizes an "arc of heaven." This heaven and earth relationship is often shown in conjunction with the Sacred Law as a representation of God's heavenly and earthly creations. These three Great Lights are highly regarded by Freemasons as symbols steeped in revelation, righteousness, and redemption.

THE FIRST STONE OF THE TEMPLE

In the masonry trade, the northeast corner holds a special place, as it marks the spot where the first stone, or cornerstone, of a building is placed. Symbolically, an Entered Apprentice takes his place during the ceremony in the northeast corner of the room, signifying that from that spot he will build his own temple according to the principles of the Brotherhood.

There are several interpretations of the significance of the northeast positioning of an Apprentice. In Freemasonry, north represents darkness while east represents light, which makes the northeast corner the midpoint between the darkness and the light. It is also said that this light/dark dichotomy is reflective of the equal balance of night and day during the Spring equinox.

GET A CLUE!

The importance traditionally assigned to the cornerstone of a building dates back to the Old Testament, specifically the Book of Psalms. The cornerstone is buried beneath the ground to represent the building's initial step out of its earthly plane toward the heavens. «

Some contain vaults in which buried treasures or talismans can be preserved as symbols of hope for the building's future. Masons often inserted time capsules. In *The Lost Symbol,* the lost word (which actually refers to the Bible) was buried in the cornerstone of the Washington Monument, laid on July 4, 1848, in a full Masonic ritual.

Initiation of the Second Degree: Fellowcraft

The second degree, or Fellowcraft, marks an individual's spiritual ascendance into adulthood in the Craft. Like the Entered

Apprentice the Fellowcraft degree is highly symbolic, but in ways that illuminate, grant passage, and offer instruction and elevation toward "the East." The second degree is about advancement, assuming new responsibilities, and using the Three Great Lights to further an individual's connection to the Brotherhood.

The primary symbol of the second degree, a winding staircase, leads to the "Middle Chamber of the Temple." The seven steps symbolize the Seven Liberal Arts and Sciences:

- Grammar
- Logic
- Rhetoric
- Arithmetic
- Geometry
- Astronomy
- Music

Other symbols also mark an individual's ascension, including ladders, staircases, mountains, and vertical ropes. Additional benefits (wages symbolically represented by corn, wine, and oil) are offered to Fellowcraft initiates, and their working tools—the square, the level, and plumb—become instruments used for testing purposes in order to ascertain the true from the false.

THE MAGICAL NUMBER 3

The number 3 is a revered number in Freemasonry as it relates to groupings, science, history, and especially geometry. This is first introduced in the second degree and, like most Masonic symbols, implies deeper meaning than the obvious.

As the Entered Apprentice symbolically focuses on the body, the Fellowcraft focuses on the mind and perfection of faculties through the mediums of art and science. The teachings of this degree are profound, as they allow initiates entrance into new areas of the Brotherhood and further education into the symbolism associated with a Fellowcraft Mason.

GET A CLUE!

The word *talisman* derives from the Greek word *telesma*, meaning "complete." A talisman is an object imbued with magical powers. (Or at least someone believes it is.) The talisman may possess magical abilities, such as bringing luck or love or warding off evil.

Believers use talismans to conduct spiritual rituals. In *The Lost Symbol*, Robert Langdon has been in possession of a talisman that he keeps in the sealed package it arrived in. That talisman turns out to be a key to revealing the puzzle at the heart of the story. «

THE SQUARE, THE LEVEL, AND THE PLUMB

The Apprentice learns that the square symbolizes earth. It is plain, its sides are of equal measure, and it is used for testing angles. The Fellowcraft initiate increases his awareness of the square as a symbol representing honesty, morality, and truthfulness. Two sides of a square form a right angle, mimicking stones used to build strong upright structures. The square is accurate but the angle is such that it forces one to follow the correct path.

The level by its very nature is symbolic of spiritual balance and equality. It is meant to show that though all men may not be on equal ground, they all have the opportunity to achieve greatness. The plumb represents rectitude or "uprightness of conduct." Thought of in terms of a plumb line, it is said to relate to justice: all individuals shouldn't be judged by the standards of others, only by their own sense of right and wrong.

The Pillars of Solomon

Other important symbols introduced to Fellowcraft initiates are the pillars on the porch, which are historically linked to the Temple of Solomon. These two pillars, which represent power and control, were located at the porchway, or entrance, to the Temple, and it is speculated that globes atop the columns alternately represent the celestial (heaven) and terrestrial (earth) respectively.

TWO PILLARS PLUS ONE

The two pillars at the entrance to Solomon's Temple actually have names. The pillar on the left is called *Boaz*, and the pillar on the right is named *Jachin*.

It is said that the pillars also relate to the Three Great Supports of Masonry. Wisdom (south) and strength (north) denote the pair of columns, and the potential Fellowcraftsman at his initiation is a third column, which symbolizes balance or beauty.

ASCENDING TO THE DIVINE TRUTH

The winding staircase is the primary symbol associated with the second degree. It is said that eighteenth-century Masons adopted the symbol from the First Book of Kings, which makes reference to the middle chamber.

While the Entered Apprentice is but a child in the Craft, the Fellowcraftsman, when standing before the winding staircase, begins the life of a man by passing through the pillars on the porch and starting his ascent of the stairs in ultimate pursuit of the Divine Truth to which all Masons aspire. It is said that with each step, he strives to improve himself, taking careful notes of the symbols surrounding him, and learn as much as his journey through life provides. The reward for successfully completing this intellectual and moral quest is heightened character and ascension into a higher life. It is a difficult passage made successful with instruction and ultimate wisdom.

HOMER THE GREAT MASON, ER, STONECUTTER

In a 1995 episode of *The Simpsons* titled "Homer the Great," Masonry makes an appearance when Homer becomes a member of the Springfield chapter of the Sacred Order of the Stonecutters. His initiation ceremony is replete with symbols of Freemasonry, including a square and compass, and an eye within a triangle. In true *Simpsons* fashion, the initiation closes with the following declaration:

"The Sacred Order of the Stonecutters has, since ancient times, split the rocks of ignorance that obscures the light of knowledge and truth. Now let's all get drunk and play ping-pong."

During the course of his initiation, the brethren discover that Homer has the birthmark of the "Chosen One," which is a birthmark shaped like a pair of hammers. He is then appointed Grand Exalted Leader.

To join this millennia-old fraternity, a member either has to be the son of a Stonecutter or save the life of one. Part of Homer's symbolic initiation ritual is a "leap of faith" off a five-story building. The trio of rituals that follow are "Crossing the Desert," the "Unblinking Eye," and the "Paddling of the Swollen Ass."

The Fellowcraftsman is first introduced to geometry in his studies of the Seven Liberal Arts and Sciences, but in that particular science, his studies must be furthered. Because geometry is heavily entrenched in the trade of masonry, it is recognized for its importance in the symbolism of Freemasonry. Its mathematical and metaphysical origins, which date back to ancient Egyptian and Greek eras, provide an initiate with an enormous amount of information to ponder and from which to draw conclusions. The combined principles of numbering, ordering, proportion, and symmetry are all a part of geometry, and that makes the science a powerful entity that is further revealed to those pursuing the third degree.

IT'S IN THE LETTERS AND NUMBERS
Both the letter G and the number 3 are significant symbols for Freemasons. In the Greek and Hebrew alphabets, where letters are assigned numeric values, the letter G is equal to the number 3.

Initiation of the Third Degree: Master Mason

An initiate entering into the third degree will have bestowed upon him the central mystery of Freemasonry, which refers to the soul and its arrival at perfection. Commonly called the "Crown of the Blue Lodge Masonry," the degree of Master Mason is a culmination of all the teachings an individual has absorbed during the first two degrees and another step toward attaining fraternal enlightenment. Those completing the third degree are also entitled to a Masonic funeral as well as rights of relief (charity) and visitation (to other lodges).

For his tenacity in achieving the first two degrees, the Master Mason is rewarded full symbolic use of all the working tools of the trade. The trowel in particular holds special meaning for the Master, as it relates to the spread of "brotherly love." The third degree is characterized as the "sublime climax of symbolic Freemasonry." In keeping with this, an initiate into the third degree is raised to the Sublime Degree of Master Mason. Once raised, a brother can remain at this level or continue his studies of the Craft by joining one of its appendant bodies.

It is said that by this stage of Brotherly evolution, an individual has learned to balance his inner nature, developed stability, purified his physicality, and broadened his mental faculties. The beginning of the initiation rite of the Master Mason is similar to that of the previous degrees, yet worlds apart. He enters the lodge in darkness, but for this rite he is fully prepared to enter sacred territory. Fortunately, he is given the tools to do so.

THE GRAND MASTER'S TRINITY

Central to the initiation rite of the Master Mason is a symbolic dramatic enactment that brings the Temple of Solomon and the Legend of Hiram Abiff to the forefront. Often mentioned in the rituals of the Brotherhood are the three Grand Masters involved in the building of Solomon's Temple. The first is Solomon, the king of Israel; the second is his friend, the king of Tyre; and the third is architect and Master Mason Hiram Abiff, whom the Tyrian king sent to Solomon to help construct the Temple. These three Grand Masters serve to represent the Divine Truth, which all Brothers strive to achieve.

During this enactment, the Master initiate plays the role of Hiram Abiff, a man of mystical and highly symbolic meaning within the Craft. Hiram's death, at the hands of three ruffians seeking to obtain the Divine Truth, is a symbolic representation of man's ignorance, passion, and attitude—virtues he seeks to quell. Hiram's death and the fact that he took Divine secrets with him left a void in the search for ultimate enlightenment. His resurrection and reburial, however, is an allegory that denotes ultimate victory and immortality. Masonic ties to the Divine Truth are strong, and an initiate's participation in this drama serves to reinforce one of the primary beliefs of the Brotherhood.

Symbols of the Master Mason

Like the previous two initiation rites, the ceremony of the Master Mason is blanketed in symbolism. With a rich historic legacy from which to draw, the Master learns the deeper meanings of these symbols and how they apply to his spiritual journey of the Craft. The gavel, twenty-four-inch gauge, and setting maul are part of the Master's working tools, and a sprig of acacia is used as an ancient symbol of rebirth.

Emblems introduced during the rites of the Master are rife with meaning. A pot of incense signifies purity of heart, prayer, and meditation. The beehive is representative of industry and the need for constant work for the good of mankind, and the Book of Constitutions serves to remind initiates of law and morality. Also part of the rite is the Sword Pointing to a Naked Heart, which singles out the need for justice in heart and in practice. The all-seeing eye is also apparent, as it reinforces the presence of God.

THE TRIADS OF EUCLID

The Forty-Seventh Problem of Euclid is a symbol that finds its roots in Egyptian legend. It is a triad linking Osiris (vertical) to Isis (horizontal) and Horus (the diagonal).

Three additional symbols are featured in the Master Mason ritual. The anchor and the ark focus on well-being and stability in a life that is truthful and faithful. The hourglass symbolizes time and how quickly life passes, as does the scythe, which furthers the element of time and ultimately severs the cord of life, thereby presenting man to eternity.

Conclusion

The Freemasons remain an enigmatic group that intrigues everyone from cartoon characters like Homer Simpson to best-selling authors like Dan Brown with its rituals, traditions, and ceremonies—all designed to transfer the secrets of the Ancient Mysteries to new generations.

As we'll see in Chapter 5, the New World was a perfectly logical—and inspired—place for the Brotherhood to transplant the wisdom of the ages.

CHAPTER 5

THE SECRET REVOLUTION OF AMERICA

The United States of America may still be young in relation to other nations of the world, but thanks to the Freemasons who brought their esoteric heritage with them to the New World, our country is as rich in ritual, tradition, and symbolism as any other place on earth.

As we'll see, the practice of American Freemasonry differs from its European counterparts, but its fraternal ties remain strong whether the climate is revolutionary, industrial, or modernized. Eighteenth-century Americans took great care in assembling their New World brethren, while at the same time reaffirming the legends, rituals, and historic and spiritual teachings of the Craft.

All-American Freemasonry

The study of Freemasonry in the United States is in many ways a tour of early American history. Legendary individuals such as Benjamin Franklin, John Hancock, and George Washington, and events surrounding the American Revolution, including the Boston Tea Party and the signings of the Declaration of Independence and United States Constitution, are all part of the story. A European fraternity taking root in the New World is no surprise, but the journey it has taken from infancy to adulthood has proven to be fascinating through all its successes and turbulent times.

THE OLDEST FREEMASON GRAVE IN THE NEW WORLD

The earliest evidence of Freemasonry in the New World may be a flat stone slab found in the Annapolis Basin of Nova Scotia, on the shore of Goat Island. The stone bears the year 1606, and it contains an image of a square and compass. It is thought to be the gravestone of a French stonemason who had settled in the area in 1605.

In contrast to its European brethren, American Freemasonry has an historical advantage in that its origins are slightly easier to establish, but as with all things related to a secret society, there are dozens of theories and conspiracies waiting in the wings.

THE NEW JERSEY CONNECTION

One of the first recorded Freemasons in America was a Scotsman named John Skene, whose name appeared twenty-seventh on a 1670 roster of Aberdeen Lodge No. 1 in Scotland. Skene, who settled on a plantation in Mt. Holly, New Jersey, in 1682, was a Quaker who served as Deputy Governor of the Colony of West Jersey from 1685 to 1690.

Freemason Lodges in the New World

Around 1701, Londoner Daniel Coxe, a student of medicine and law, arrived in Burlington, New Jersey, where he became active in local politics and served in various governmental capacities. On June 5, 1730, Coxe was awarded an historic position in American Masonry when the Duke of Norfolk, Grand Master of the Grand Lodge of England, appointed Coxe Provincial Grand Master of the Provinces of New York, New Jersey, and Pennsylvania.

A LOCK OF GEORGE WASHINGTON'S HAIR

In 1799, upon the death of George Washington, the Grand Lodge of Massachusetts made an unusual request of his widow. In deference to their wishes, she gave them a lock of her husband's hair. Sealed in a gold urn made by silversmith Paul Revere, its safekeeping is charged to all Grand Masters upon their appointment.

Another leading American Mason was Henry Price. There is little known about Price before he emigrated to Boston from London, but records show that he was a successful merchant tailor and a Freemason. Clearly a man on a fraternal mission, he set off for England from Boston in 1732 in order to secure a warrant from the Grand Lodge of England, which was required in order to make a lodge official. His mission was a success. English Grand Master Lord Viscount Montague named Price Provincial Grand Master of New England, which gave him the authority to establish charters in New England. A year after he became Grand Master, his position was expanded to include all of North America.

On July 30, 1733, a group of Boston Masons met with Price at the Bunch of Grapes Tavern, at which point Price selected officers for America's first Grand Lodge. Now the oldest official lodge in the Western world, it was named St. John's Lodge. When his authority expanded, Price granted a petition from Benjamin Franklin and the contingent of Philadelphia Freemasons to form their lodge, of which Franklin served as their first Master. Over the years, Price continued chartering many lodges all over the colonies, and several in Canada, Dutch Guiana, and the West Indies.

As with most membership-based organizations, however, it was only a matter of time before rivalry reared its eternal head. At that point, members of the fraternal order were generally men of means—business owners, merchants, manufacturers, and individuals based in art and science. The working class was often omitted from joining the Brotherhood. As such, working individuals formed their Grand Lodge under the auspices of following traditional Masonic practices. This, as it's been told, led to a great divide among brethren that saw lodges bitterly divided between ancient and modern groups.

Benjamin Franklin: The Lightning Rod of Masonry

Arguably one of the most famous and industrious Americans is Benjamin Franklin. An inventor, printer, scientist, philosopher, author, and exceptional diplomat and statesman, Franklin is revered not only by posterity, but also by his fellow brethren both past and present. Coming from a man with only two years of formal education, Franklin's achievements in the colonies and as a diplomat abroad were nothing short of astounding. From 1729 to 1765 he edited and published the *Pennsylvania Gazette*. He also learned several languages, formed the first police force in the colonies, introduced hospital services, founded the first public library, and is credited with a wide range of inventions, including the lightning rod and bifocals.

In 1753, Franklin was appointed postmaster general and four years later moved to England to serve as the chief representative of the American colonies. By the time he returned to America more than a decade later, despite his efforts in Britain to find redress for the colonists' grievances, the American

Revolution had begun. As a member of the Second Continental Congress, he served on a committee of five individuals who were chosen to draft the Declaration of Independence. Franklin was also a key player in obtaining funds from France's Louis XVI for the young republic, and he eventually helped negotiate a commerce and alliance treaty with France that helped turn the tide of the American Revolution.

NECESSITY IS THE MASON OF INVENTION

After Benjamin Franklin invented the furnace stove, he created the first fire company and fire insurance company. As postmaster, in an effort to better calculate routes of service, Franklin invented an odometer, which he attached to his carriage.

In 1730, Franklin made mention of several Freemason lodges in the *Gazette*. Shortly thereafter, he became a member of the St. John's Lodge. Six months later, on St. John the Baptist's Day of 1732, he became Junior Warden of the Grand Lodge in Pennsylvania, only to be chosen Grand Master two years later. A free thinker, Franklin then began his correspondence in an effort to secure a Masonic charter.

The majority of Franklin's lodge gatherings were held in Philadelphia at Tun's Tavern and also in a Videll Alley building. It was in the latter in 1786 that the Grand Lodge of Free and Accepted Masons of Pennsylvania declared its independence from the Grand Lodge of England. Franklin continued his long and extraordinary career as a diplomat and trailblazer of the American Brotherhood. Near the end of his life, he was still fighting for a cause, this time the abolition of slavery.

Franklin died not long after he played a significant part in writing and ratifying the United States Constitution, but his multifaceted legacies continue to thrive.

The Boston Tea Party

One might wonder what the infamous Boston Tea Party has to do with Freemasonry. As it turns out, there's quite a Masonic mystery attached to the notorious tea dumping that set the stage for the American Revolution.

As history tells it, the phrase "no taxation without representation" became a mantra for colonists who were angered over the 1765 Stamp Act and the Townshend Acts of 1767. One of the loudest protesters was Freemason John Hancock, who later organized a boycott of tea from the British East India Company.

Although the British government passed the Tea Act, which eliminated the colonial tea tax, ships continued to be turned away from American ports. Then on the night of December 16, 1773, a group of Bostonians calling themselves the Sons of Liberty boarded the ships *Dartmouth, Eleanor,* and *Beaver.* Disguised as Mohawk Indians, they dumped 342 crates of tea into Boston Harbor, after which they swept the decks clean and made certain all the tea aboard the ships had been destroyed. The Sons of Liberty were named the perpetrators of this act of political protest.

STILL OPEN FOR BUSINESS: THE GREEN DRAGON TAVERN

The Green Dragon Tavern is still standing at 11 Marshall Street in Boston, Massachusetts. Although no longer a Masonic lodge, it does still serve beer and food such as Mohawk Trail chicken fingers and Red Coat spicy buffalo wings.

No one knows with any certainty who actually conceived of the infamous raid, so one legend is as good as another. One alternate claim to the Boston Tea Party boasts a significant Masonic spin. In this case, connection to the brethren starts with the Green Dragon Tavern, a building that was purchased by the St. Andrew's Lodge in 1764. Sometimes dubbed the "Headquarters of the American Revolution," the downstairs tavern and upstairs meeting rooms were said to have served the Grand Lodge of Massachusetts as well as the Sons of Liberty.

Allegedly, the Tea Party was planned at the Green Dragon and executed with the help of the Masons. Involved in the planning were Grand Master Dr. Joseph Warren, and fellow brethren John Hancock and Paul Revere. It was, in fact, Warren who sent his good friend Revere on his infamous ride to warn colonial troops of British incursion on April 18, 1775. And the men Revere delivered his messages to? Revolutionary Samuel Adams and Freemason John Hancock.

The American Revolution

Like most aspects of Freemasonry, participation of the brethren in the Boston Tea Party remains a source of debate. There are all kinds of intriguing conspiracy theories based on various allegations that all the founding fathers and all of George Washington's generals were part of the Craft. Some assert that the majority of signers of both the Declaration of Independence and United States Constitution were Masons

What is known is that many Freemasons took part in the Revolutionary War. Masonic brethren served as military leaders, soldiers, politicians, patriots, revolutionaries, and statesmen, but in general, their numbers were small as compared to the non-Masons who participated in the war. Much of the speculation and subsequent conspiracies surrounding Masonic involvement is perhaps due to the fact that a handful of highly influential individuals were indeed Masons.

WERE THOMAS JEFFERSON, PATRICK HENRY, AND SAMUEL ADAMS FREEMASONS?

Although these three men are often listed as members of the Craft, there is no evidence that any of them were ever initiated into the fraternity. Adams was a close associate of Paul Revere and John Hancock, who were well-known Masons. Jefferson also had documented Masonic connections, but Henry did not.

Due to their stature or famous incidents involving them, men such as George Washington, Benjamin Franklin, John Hancock, Paul Revere, John Paul Jones, Ethan Allen, Baron von Steuben, and the Marquis de Lafayette brought Freemasonry to the forefront simply by association. The same goes for infamous Masons such as Benedict Arnold and Major John André.

Founding Fathers

It is a common misconception that all of the founding fathers of the United States were Masons. This is hardly the case. It is true that many prominent Masons took part in the war and at least twenty signed the Declaration and Constitution, but there were many more non-Masons who participated in these events.

MASONS, MASONS EVERYWHERE

In his book *The Secret Teachings of All Ages*, Manly P. Hall claims that the United States was actually a grand Masonic "experiment" to create a new society that would one day grow to such prominence that it would allow the Masons to dominate the world. No fewer than fourteen U.S. presidents have been Masons.

Those given to conspiracy often claim that the U.S. Constitution is based on James Anderson's *The Constitutions of Free-*

Masons. They also attribute Masonic connections to individuals like Thomas Jefferson and Patrick Henry, who have never been part of the Craft. Another popular myth is that every one of the generals serving under George Washington during the war was a Freemason. In truth only thirty-three Masons served under Washington's command.

Another common conspiracy theory holds that when Washington was inaugurated as president, all of the governors of the original thirteen colonies were Freemasons. Research shows that of the thirty individuals who served as governors during the colonial period, only ten were members of the Craft.

THE DECLARATION OF INDEPENDENCE: A *NATIONAL TREASURE*

In the film *National Treasure*, starring Nicolas Cage, the Declaration of Independence contains a clue that leads to a treasure trove the Knights Templar procured and the Freemasons kept hidden. Cage's character, incidentally, is named Benjamin Franklin Gates.

Perhaps the single most important document in American history is the Declaration of Independence. On July 4, 1776, the document was ratified by the Continental Congress, and in its eloquence stated, with apt justification, that the thirteen colonies were declaring themselves independent of the Kingdom of Britain. A committee of five men were responsible for the writing of the Declaration, one of whom was Mason Benjamin Franklin.

A total of fifty-six delegates ultimately signed the famous declaration, and of those, nine were Freemasons:

- William Ellery, member of the First Lodge of Boston
- Benjamin Franklin, Grand Master of Pennsylvania

- John Hancock, who became a Mason in the Merchant's Lodge No. 277 in Quebec, and then moved to St. Andrew's Lodge in Boston
- Joseph Hewes, member of the Unanimity Lodge No. 7 in North Carolina
- William Hopper, member of the Hanover Lodge in Masonborough, North Carolina
- Robert Treat Payne, member of the Massachusetts Grand Lodge
- Richard Stockton, Charter Master of St. John's Lodge in Princeton, New Jersey
- George Walton, member of Solomon's Lodge No. 1, in Savannah, Georgia
- William Whipple, member of St. John's Lodge in Portsmouth, New Hampshire

By 1787, the time had arrived to create a governmental structure for the newly independent nation, and a number of Freemasons played an integral part in the process. The Constitutional Convention was held in May in Philadelphia, and after a unanimous vote by the fifty-five delegates, George Washington became presiding officer. Also in attendance as a delegate was octogenarian Benjamin Franklin.

THE NUMBER ONE MASONIC SIGNATORY: JOHN HANCOCK

Freemason Hancock, a statesman who served as president of the Continental Congress, was the first signatory of the Declaration of Independence. His signature was very large as compared to the others. Legend has it that Hancock did that intentionally so that King George III could clearly read his signature.

Extensive debate led to the eventual creation of the United States Constitution, and of the five primary men leading the debate—Washington, Franklin, John Adams, Thomas Jefferson, and Edmund Randolph—only Adams and Jefferson were non-Masons. The document was to replace the Articles of Confederation and create a federal union of sovereign states and a federal government. After being ratified in each of the thirteen states, it became official on March 4, 1789.

Out of the original thirty-nine individuals who signed the Constitution (fifty-five was the eventual total of those who signed), thirteen were Freemasons. Known Masons who signed include:

- Gunning Bedford Jr., the first Grand Master of Delaware
- John Blair, the first Grand Master of Virginia
- David Brearley, the first Grand Master of New Jersey
- Jacob Broom, an officer in his lodge in Delaware
- Daniel Carroll, the Maryland Mason who with George Washington participated in the Masonic cornerstone laying of the United States Capitol building
- Jonathan Dayton, a member of Temple Lodge No. 1 in Elizabethtown, New Jersey
- John Dickinson, a lodge member in Dover, Delaware
- Benjamin Franklin, Grand Master of Pennsylvania
- Nicholas Gilman, a member of St. John's Lodge No. 1, Portsmouth, New Hampshire
- Rufus King, a member of the St. John's Lodge in Newburyport, Massachusetts
- James McHenry, a member of Spiritual Lodge No. 23 in Maryland

- William Paterson, a member of Trenton Lodge No. 5 in New Jersey
- George Washington, who originally joined the lodge at Fredericksburg (now Fredericksburg Lodge No. 4), Charter Master of Alexandria Lodge No. 22, in Virginia

A Commanding Mason: George Washington

George Washington is known and revered by all American citizens as a brilliant military leader, statesman, founding father, and the first president of the United States. Washington is also famous for being a Freemason, a fact that inspires pride in all of his American brethren. It wasn't so much that he was heavily involved in the Craft, but that he was steadfast in his moral virtue. Oddly, Washington's participation in the Brotherhood is a source of debate, with some theorizing that he never was a Mason. Happily, this matter is easily resolved.

Records from the lodge at Fredericksburg, Virginia (which is still in possession of the records), show that Washington was initiated as an Entered Apprentice on November 4, 1752, and further became a Fellowcraftsman on March 3, 1753. By the following August, he was raised to the Sublime Degree of Master Mason. It has also been speculated that Washington further went on to earn the Royal Arch degree.

WELL-DISPOSED TO THE CRAFT

In response to an address from the Grand Lodge of Massachusetts, it is said that Washington stated, "My attachment to the Society of which we are members will dispose me always to contribute my best endeavors to promote the honor and prosperity of the Craft."

By 1775, Washington was unanimously chosen commander-in-chief of the Colonial Army. At the Federal Convention in Philadelphia in May of 1787, Washington presided as the United States Constitution was framed. On April 30, 1789, Washington was sworn in as first president of the United States by fellow Mason Robert Livingston, the chancellor of New York, and Grand Master of Free and Accepted Masons.

The year before his presidential victory, Washington was appointed Master of Alexandria Lodge No. 22 in Virginia. Later that year he was elected Master but no records exist of his presiding over any lodge. When Washington passed away on December 14, 1799, he received, at his widow's request, a Masonic funeral.

Black Sheep Brother: Benedict Arnold

Like most organizations, the Brotherhood is not without its infamous members. One individual in particular is so reviled that the mere utterance of his name on American soil is synonymous with treason. Benedict Arnold, a brother shown to have been initiated into the Brotherhood in New Haven, Connecticut, in 1765, served as a general in the Continental Army during the American Revolution.

A former druggist and bookseller turned West Indies trader, Arnold was ambitious and increasingly aware of the British presence in the New World. For the first part of his military career Arnold served with distinction until his command was given to another by the Continental Congress after the Battle of Ticonderoga in 1775. Arnold's bitterness over that decision, made worse by future altercations, would later result in his defection to the British military and, in 1780, his plan to deliver the American fort at West Point, New York, to British control. Arnold's plot proved unsuccessful, but for the effort he was monetarily rewarded and made brigadier general in the British Army. Fellow Masonic Brother and conspirator Major John André was not so lucky.

A British Army soldier at the age of twenty-one, André found his way to Canada, where he was captured. He was returned to Pennsylvania and held prisoner until 1776, when he was part of a prisoner exchange between the British and American armies. Two years later he was commissioned as a major in the British army and became a popular individual in New York and Philadelphia society. At one point he even lived in the house of fellow Mason Benjamin Franklin. By 1780, however, Major André's destiny would turn when he entered into Benedict Arnold's West Point plot.

A TASTE FOR WOMEN—AND TREASON
General Arnold and Major André had more in common than just Freemasonry. In 1779, Arnold met and married eighteen-year-old Peggy Shippen, who, during the British occupation of Philadelphia, was being courted by Major André!

After meeting with Arnold, André was dispatched carrying documents meant for the British, which told how the fort could be taken. Unfortunately for the major, his endeavor proved futile as he was captured, tried as a spy, and hanged. The British viewed André as a gallant officer, and in 1821 his remains were moved to the famed "Hero's Corner" at Westminster Abbey in London.

The William Morgan Mystery

In the history of American Freemasonry, there is perhaps no more intriguing a tale than the mysterious demise of William Morgan. The mix of circumstances, evidence, hearsay, public speculation, and alleged abduction and murder weave a fantastic tale perfect for a made-for-television movie. The fact that the case was so much in the public eye is arguably the most crucial element of the mystery, since the eventual outrage and exposure of the Brotherhood and its secrecy led to widespread anti-Mason sentiments and the formation of the Anti-Masonic Party.

A native of Culpepper County in Virginia, William Morgan left his home to spend time working various jobs in Canada and areas of New York. In 1824, Morgan settled in the small town of Batavia, New York, and began work as an itinerant stonemason. Referring to himself as "Captain" Morgan, he cited his distinctive military service in the War of 1812.

Whether Morgan actually did serve in the armed forces is still questioned by historians, and many accounts of the Morgan mystery vary widely.

Some historical accounts show that in 1825 in the Western Star Chapter No. 33 in LeRoy, New York, Morgan was awarded a Royal Arch degree. Experts disagree as to whether he was ever really a Mason (most assert he wasn't) or had simply lied his way into the fraternity for his own evil gain. Other accounts tell that Morgan showed up at the lodge claiming he was already a brother, which incited suspicion among that lodge's brethren.

No matter whether he was a true Mason or not, several accounts state that Morgan spent time visiting other lodges and eventually was part of a group that was petitioning for a Royal Arch Chapter (a division of the York Rite). However, when the chapter was started, Morgan was denied membership. Unbeknownst to everyone, this marked the beginning of a powerful public scandal that would shock brethren around the world.

MORGAN SPILLS FREEMASON SECRETS

Morgan's omission from the new Batavian charter group resulted in arguments, and Morgan left the fraternity. At that point, he made his intentions clear: he was writing a book that would reveal all the secrets of Freemasonry—including their rituals and procedures—and he had, in fact, been paid a great sum in advance of the book by David Miller, publisher of a local newspaper, the *Batavia Advocate*. Morgan's contract for the book involved Miller, a Mason who for twenty years did not progress beyond Entered Apprentice and bore a grudge against the Brotherhood; Morgan's landlord, John Davids; and a man called Russell Dyer.

Morgan exacerbated the issue by continually boasting about the enormous sum he had been paid for the book, which only gave rise to anger among the brethren. In order to avert the potential crisis, local Masons ran advertisements in other publications, which informed the public to be watchful of Morgan and his undesirable attributes.

As one historian tells the tale, shortly thereafter, a local innkeeper was asked by a Mason to provide a meal for fifty of his brethren, who revealed that their intention that evening was to attack the *Batavia Advocate*'s offices. After hearing of their plan, Miller put out the word that he and others were armed and prepared for any attack. The Freemasons never executed their plan, but the incident did set off a chain of events.

It is said that several Masons approached Morgan at his residence and arrested him for debts he owed them. He was taken to a local jail in the charge of a jailer who also happened to be a Mason. Miller, upon hearing of Morgan's incarceration, set about finding the jailer so as to pay off Morgan's alleged debt; however, it was a Friday evening and the jailer had conveniently departed, leaving Morgan behind bars until Monday.

With the jailer absent, the Freemasons returned to confront Morgan about his scandalous exposé, telling him that if he gave them the book he would go free. After he refused to do so, they went to his home and engaged in a futile attempt to recover Morgan's work. From there, matters only got worse.

By Monday morning, Miller paid Morgan's "debt," and he was released. The Freemasons then turned around and had him immediately arrested for stealing a shirt and tie and owing another small debt in the town of Canandaigua, about fifty miles east of Batavia. He was driven there in a carriage and again incarcerated. At the same time, an unsuccessful attempt was made to jail Miller.

A MASONIC KIDNAPPING

On September 13, 1826, a man claiming to be Morgan's friend showed up at the jail to pay the alleged debt and secure the prisoner's release. Lotan Lawson, Morgan's "friend," spoke with the jailer's wife, who cleared the charge and released a highly suspicious Morgan from his captivity. Once outside the building, Lawson supposedly insisted that Morgan join him in his carriage, at which point two Freemasons called Chesebro and Sawyer forced the reluctant man into the coach. It is said that those who witnessed the encounter heard Morgan shout "Murder!" as the carriage disappeared from sight.

ONLY A MISDEMEANOR

When the Morgan affair took place, kidnapping was a mere misdemeanor in the State of New York. Governor DeWitt Clinton, a Mason, as a result of the Morgan affair, later signed a bill elevating the punishment to up to fourteen years.

Where the carriage traveled for the next two days is a source of speculation, but investigators later attested that Morgan and his kidnappers made their way over 100 miles from Canandaigua to Fort Niagara (between the United States and Canada). At some point the kidnappers were joined by Freemason and High Sheriff of Niagara County Eli Bruce and made a stop in the town of Youngstown, where witnesses heard Morgan inside the carriage.

DID MORGAN'S EXPOSÉ FUEL ANTI-MASONRY?

David Miller printed William Morgan's book and sold each copy for one dollar. By the time he produced the second edition, competition had forced his price down to fifty cents as dozens of books rolled off the presses, "exposing" Freemasonry. The flood of anti-Mason propaganda continued down through the years. By 1932 there were well over 100 anti-Masonic newspapers in print in the United States.

The fort at Niagara, which formerly contained the federal government's department of defense, was empty when the carriage arrived on September 14. Investigators later asserted that the fort's caretaker (who was a Mason) granted the kidnappers access. For the next few days, Morgan was held inside the fort. It is said that at one point four Freemasons took him by boat across the river to the Canadian border. According to a ferryman, a meeting between several American and Canadian Masons ensued, at which time the American men were willing to transfer Morgan to their cohorts to eliminate him by undetermined means. No plan was apparently agreed upon, and Morgan was returned to the fort and never again seen.

THE DISAPPEARING BODY OF MORGAN

Back in Batavia rumors, innuendo, and accusations were spreading. Friends of Morgan were alerting the press to his absence, as others were asserting that in order to prevent his book from being published, the Freemasons had murdered him. Smelling the makings of what became an immediate bestseller, publisher David Miller took the opportunity to promote Morgan's book.

Those who believed that Morgan had been murdered theorized that when the Canadian Masons refused to take Morgan, the kidnappers weighted his legs and tossed him into the Niagara River. Another theory suggested he was taken over the Canadian border and given a horse and five hundred dollars to disappear. The Freemasons countered that Morgan and Miller had concocted the entire event in order to generate fervor over Morgan's exposé. In an effort to quell growing public outrage over the event, past Grand Master and now New York Governor DeWitt Clinton offered a $300 dollar reward for Morgan's return or information concerning his disappearance.

MORGAN'S "WIDOW" "MARRIES" MORMON FOUNDER JOSEPH SMITH

After the disappearance of her husband, William Morgan's wife, Lucinda, became heavily involved in the anti-Masonic movement. In 1830 she married anti-Mason George W. Harris and then became intimately involved with Joseph Smith, founder of the Mormon Church. Records show that while Lucinda was still married to Harris, she was also "sealed," or married, to Smith, who was later murdered in 1844 in Nauvoo, Illinois, by an anti-Mormon mob.

The public outcry increased when a body washed ashore on the banks of the Niagara River several weeks later. At first it was believed to be Morgan, and an inquest identified it as him. However, a second inquest refuted that decision when rumors of inconsistent markings on his body were touted. A Canadian woman speculated that the body might be that of her missing husband. At a third inquest the woman definitively identified the body as that of her husband, and the matter was laid to rest.

When all was said and done, and without a body to prove murder, kidnappers Lawson, Bruce, Chesebro, Sawyer, and another Mason called Sheldon were convicted of Morgan's abduction. Protests ensued over the leniency of their sentences and imprisonment, which ranged from one month to just over two years.

Birth of the Anti-Masonic Party

The Morgan Affair began an anti-Masonic fervor that would not be easily subdued. Freemasons in general to this day maintain that Morgan was not murdered but instead struck a financial deal with the American Masons and, with the help of Canadian Freemasons, disappeared into obscurity. A wide measure of theories have been put forward since the incident, but no one can say with any certainty what really happened to William Morgan.

What can be said is that anti-Masonic sentiment continued to grow at an alarming rate, with the Brotherhood falling under close public scrutiny. Several anti-Mason meetings were held in 1828, which set forth a cycle that focused on everything from the secrecy of the fraternity to the alleged blood oaths in which they participate.

Persecution of the Brotherhood

The sociopolitical climate at the time of the Morgan Affair was tumultuous, and a measure of this discontent manifested itself in a third political party called the Anti-Masonic Party. Much of its fury was directed at Andrew Jackson, who was enormously popular and the most prominent Democrat in the country. Though he failed to win the presidency in 1824, his stature was unscathed and he was set to once again run for office in 1828. A lawyer, statesman, and military leader, Jackson was also a Freemason—a Grand Master of the lodges of Tennessee. Naturally, this added fuel to the fire.

The Anti-Masonic Party grew quickly. Several of its candidates even held governorships in Vermont and Pennsylvania. Political and social campaigns against Masons were bitter affairs, and as persecution in society took hold, many Masons and their families were denied freedoms and were banned from their schools and churches. The idea that Freemasons considered themselves above the law—coupled with their secret blood rituals—was unacceptable to the public, and it created an atmosphere of paranoia. As a result, the fraternity suffered greatly.

Despite the efforts made by the Anti-Masonic Party, Jackson won his 1828 presidential campaign against Whig John Quincy Adams. Four years later, the anti-Masons elevated one of their own at a national convention and presented former Mason William Wirt of Maryland as a presidential candidate. A three-way election between Jackson, Wirt, and Whig candidate

Henry Clay gave President Jackson a decisive victory, and saw Wirt only carry the state of Vermont.

Though the Anti-Masonic Party began fading away in 1835, the damage had been done and would take more than twenty years to undo. Lodge memberships decreased by the thousands in most states, and in some cases lodges were abandoned entirely.

PRESIDENT MILLARD FILLMORE: ANTI-MASON MAKES GOOD

In his youth, Fillmore was indeed an anti-Mason. However, on July 4, 1851, during his term as thirteenth president of the United States, Fillmore invited the District of Columbia Grand Lodge to lay the cornerstone for the extension of the Capitol building.

One historian states that 227 lodges were under the Grand Lodge of New York in 1827. Eight years later, that number decreased to only forty-one. In Vermont, every lodge either gave up its charter or simply became dormant. Even the Grand Lodge stopped holding meetings for several years. This decline was also apparent in Rhode Island, Massachusetts, and Pennsylvania.

The abduction and disappearance of William Morgan set into motion a devastating chain of events for American Freemasons, but it wasn't the first time the Brotherhood had been persecuted and, like their European brethren, they would again see the Craft ascend from the ashes. Single-handedly, Albert Pike would soon revitalize and refashion American Freemasonry in general—and the Scottish rite in particular—with his controversial and influential work, *Morals And Dogma*.

Conclusion

As we've seen in this chapter, Freemasonry has influenced the course of American history from the earliest beginnings of our nation. From the Founding Fathers to Albert Pike and beyond, American Freemasonry has counted the most wealthy and powerful citizens among its members. Now let's take a closer look at the Masonic roster of the Rich and Famous in America. You may be surprised.

CHAPTER 6
THE SECRET LIVES OF
AMERICAN FREEMASONS

A list of famous Masons in the United States reads like a who's who of American history and ingenuity. Names associated with the Brotherhood run the gamut from presidents and diplomats to scientists and entertainers. Freemasonry most definitely took root and thrived in the open free-thinking environment of the New World, and its membership reflects that historical progression. From Benjamin Franklin to Bob Hope, American Masonry has enjoyed and continues to enjoy a diverse and highly innovative membership—one that impacts our government, society, and culture in myriad ways.

The Brotherhood of Achievement

Over the centuries, the Brotherhood has attracted hundreds of influential members of society, from leaders of industry to presidents to a host of entertainers and historical groundbreakers. As noted in earlier chapters, arguably one of the most well-known American Masons of his day was Benjamin Franklin, who, along with the Founding Fathers of the United States, elevated Freemasonry to prominence in the New World.

Benjamin Franklin helped bring American Masonry to the forefront of American life. With an impressive career as a diplomat, scientist, printer, writer, and philosopher, he is often considered to be one of America's finest statesmen. In 1734, he published Freemasonry's Anderson's *Constitutions*. In addition, Franklin was one of the thirteen Masons who signed the Constitution, and he served as Grand Master of Pennsylvania.

THE WICKED GOOD HANDWRITING OF JOHN HANCOCK

President of the Continental Congress and nine-term governor of Massachusetts. John Hancock is perhaps equally famous for being the first individual to sign the Declaration of Independence along with eight of his Masonic brothers.

The thrill of discovery and invention is a natural complement to the Brotherhood, where Masons seek to enhance their communities and stretch their own educational wings. Many famous Masons carry recognizable names such as Ford, Macy, and Gillette, while others, like John Fitch, may not be as well known. Fitch was the inventor of the steamboat, a discovery often attributed to Robert Fulton, who was also a Mason.

The Masonic Lights of Industry

The lure of a "secret" fraternal organization such as the Freemasons would, without a doubt, be tantalizing for those taking part in an industrial revolution. It's no wonder that so many influential movers and shakers joined the Brotherhood.

One such Mason was David Sarnoff, a Russian-born American from modest means who started his career working with the Marconi Wireless Telegraph Company in 1906. Sarnoff then worked his way into radio broadcasting at the Radio Corporation of America (RCA), where he eventually organized their

National Television Broadcasting Company. In 1929, he met Vladimir Zworykin, inventor of the all-electric camera tube, and by 1953, RCA's color television became the mainstay of many American homes.

THE HIDDEN TRUTH BEHIND HOUSEHOLD NAMES

A Mason named Lloyd Balfour may not be instantly recognizable, but for generations students have been purchasing their class rings from Balfour Jewelry. And that washing machine that works so hard for every American household? It was invented by Mason Frederick Maytag, whose company originally produced farm equipment, until he discovered a way to run the washer with an external power source.

BEHIND THE HOLLYWOOD SIGN

The film industry also included several prominent Masons. Louis B. Mayer, the man behind the eventual merge of what became Metro-Goldwyn-Mayer (MGM), was a Mason, and Jack Warner of Warner Brothers Studios was also in the Brotherhood. Also part of the fraternity was Darryl Zanuck, who in 1933 cofounded 20th Century Productions.

Several prominent car manufacturers are also on the Masonic roster, including Walter Chrysler, founder of the Chrysler Corporation; Ransom E. Olds; and perhaps the most revered automobile manufacturer in history, Henry Ford, who invented the first gasoline-powered automobile. By 1903 he founded the Ford Motor Company and began mass-producing his vehicles.

Here are two more famous Masons everyone is sure to recognize. Mason Harlan "Colonel" Sanders made his mark when he founded his "finger lickin' good" Kentucky Fried Chicken, and Dave Thomas made Wendy's restaurants a household name with the catch phrase, "Where's the beef?"

Other influential industrialist Masons include:

- Lawrence Bell of the Bell Aircraft Corporation
- Herbert H. Dow, founder of the Dow Chemical Company
- Charles C. Hilton, hotel magnate
- Rowland Hussey Macy, founder of R. H. Macy & Company, in New York
- James Cash Penney, renowned retail entrepreneur who in 1902 founded J. C. Penney

A BROTHERHOOD OF INVENTION

A host of inventors also chose to join the Brotherhood. The name King C. Gillette is instantly recognizable as the Mason who developed a type of "safety razor." As a result, he founded the Gillette Safety Razor Company. Perhaps less known, but still highly significant, is John Loudon McAdam, a Mason who invented pavement made with layers of crushed stone (a process called macadamization).

Guns, Words, and Steel

A pair of firearms aficionados were also Masons. Samuel Colt patented his revolutionary revolving pistol in America in 1836, and his Colt revolvers are still manufactured to this day. Mason Richard Jordan Gatling founded the Gatling Gun Company in 1862, which merged with Colt in 1897. The Gatling gun was America's first successful machine gun.

Inventive members of the Brotherhood include:

- John Fitch, a clockmaker, brassworker, and silversmith who in 1786 built the first recorded steam-powered ship in America
- Richard March Hoe, inventor of the rotary printing press in 1843, which revolutionized the newspaper printing industry
- Harry S. New, journalist, politician, and postmaster general who helped expand airmail service
- Simon Lake, a mechanical engineer and innovator of submarine construction who held more than 200 patents for advanced naval designs
- George Pullman, the industrialist who in 1864 invented and built the first railroad sleeper car
- Orville and Wilbur Wright, renowned brothers and the inventors of the first airplane

All the Mason's Men

Freemasonry has established an impressive legacy in the United States and has attracted a long list of powerful men. As a result, many politicians, statesmen, and individuals serving in America's military forces have belonged to the Brotherhood.

PRESIDENTIAL PRESTIGE

Fourteen United States presidents have been Masons, from George Washington to Gerald Ford. Given the high profile of their position, this gave Freemasonry an air of prestige akin to that of the Masonic royal members in Europe. Fourth president of the United States Andrew Jackson was a Mason, as was Harry Truman, and both Franklin and Theodore Roosevelt.

The following American presidents also belonged to the Masonic order:

- James Monroe, a Democratic-Republican, fifth president (1817–1825)
- James Knox Polk, a Democrat and eleventh president (1845–1849)
- James Buchanan, a Democrat and fifteenth president (1857–1861)
- Andrew Johnson, a Democrat and seventeenth president (1865–1861)
- James Garfield, a Republican and twentieth president (1881)
- William McKinley, a Republican and twenty-fifth president (1897–1901)
- William Howard Taft, a Republican and twenty-seventh president (1909–1913)
- Warren G. Harding, a Republican and twenty-ninth president (1921–1923)

ALOHA, FREEMASONS!

Also distinguishing themselves in the Craft were a host of Hawaiian royalty. Several of the Kamehameha line of kings took part in the Brotherhood, including Kamehameha the Third, Fourth, and Fifth. King David Kalahaua, the last reigning monarch of the Hawaiian Kingdom, was also a Mason.

MASONIC TRUTH AND JUSTICE FOR ALL

The Brotherhood also welcomed many statesmen of note, including Sam Houston, the first president of the Republic of Texas, and Thurgood Marshall, the first African-American

Supreme Court Justice. Best known for his leadership of the Federal Bureau of Investigation from 1924 to 1972 was Mason J. Edgar Hoover.

Statesmen who entered the Brotherhood include:

- Samuel Ervin Jr., the North Carolina Senator best known for serving on committees investigating Joe McCarthy and later Richard Nixon during the Watergate scandal
- Barry Goldwater, former Arizona Senator and 1964 Republican Party presidential candidate
- Jesse Helms, five-term conservative Senator from North Carolina
- Reverend Jesse Jackson, Baptist minister, American civil rights activist, and Democratic presidential candidate in 1984 and 1988
- Fiorello LaGuardia, former mayor of New York who served from 1934 to 1945.
- Sam Nunn, former Senator from Georgia who served for twenty-four years
- Governor George Wallace, infamous four-term governor of Alabama and presidential candidate who narrowly escaped assassination in 1972
- Earl Warren, former California district attorney, governor, and Supreme Court justice from 1953 to 1969

THE WAR ROOM OF MASONS

Dedicated men in various branches of the American military services took part in Masonry. Naval officer, explorer, and aviator Rear Admiral Richard E. Byrd is best known for his 1926 flight over the North Pole with fellow adventurer Floyd Bennet, who was also part of the Brotherhood.

Also known for his distinguished career was Scottish-born John Paul Jones, who served as first admiral of the United States Navy. And not to be outdone was Mason General Douglas MacArthur, commander of the Allied forces in the South Pacific during World War II.

AMERICA'S GREATEST MASONIC HERO

Audie Murphy was an actor, singer, and songwriter, but he is best known for having been the most decorated American combat soldier of World War II. Murphy received thirty-three awards, among them the prestigious Medal of Honor. In 1955 he became a Mason, and eventually a Shriner.

Other Masonic military leaders include:

- General Henry "Hap" Arnold, American pilot who served as first general of the U.S. Air Force
- Omar Bradley, the American general who played a crucial role in the Allied victory in World War II
- Brigadier General James Doolittle, renowned World War II Air Force pilot
- John Joseph "Black Jack" Pershing, revered army general who led American forces to victory in Germany during World War I and, in 1920, was awarded the unique rank of General of the Armies
- Eddie Rickenbacker, legendary American Air Force ace during World War I

Truth and Justice in Outer Space

The Brotherhood's zest for personal growth and exploration could likely account for their members' involvement in planetary and other-worldly discovery. Several well-known astronauts were Masons, including Neil Armstrong, the *Apollo 11* adventurer who on July 20, 1969, became the first man to walk on the moon. Fellow brother and lunar module pilot Edwin "Buzz" Aldrin became the second to take the giant leap.

Wally Schirra and Virgil "Gus" Grissom were two of the original Mercury Seven astronauts who had the right stuff. Grissom had his legendary liftoff in *Mercury 4* and splashed down in *Liberty Bell 7*, but he was killed in 1967 in a launch pad fire when commanding *Apollo 1*. Mason Schirra has the sole distinction of being the only man to fly in the first three space programs—Mercury, Gemini, and Apollo.

THE POWER OF THE POINSETTIA

Joel R. Poinsett is a Mason with a unique distinction to his credit. In 1922 Poinsett served as a special envoy to Mexico, but it is his association with a certain Christmas flower that makes him a household name. If it doesn't ring a bell yet, it will—Poinsett introduced the poinsettia into the United States.

The list of scientific and aviation Masons include:

- Charles Lindbergh, renowned aviator who piloted the first solo nonstop trans-Atlantic flight in 1927
- Dr. Charles Mayo, a Master Mason who was active in the Rochester, Minnesota, lodge and who, along with his father and brother, founded the first official medical group practices in America: the Mayo Clinic
- Albert Abraham Michelson, Prussian-born American physicist and Nobel Prize winner who in the late 1800s first measured the speed of light
- Andrew Still, the physician considered to be the father of osteopathic medicine

Also a brother is John Glenn, a former Ohio Senator and Marine fighter pilot who in 1962 became the first American to orbit earth. In 1998, Glenn made a second remarkable journey into space, securing his legacy as the oldest astronaut in history.

The Ancient Mysteries of the Arts and Athletics

The variety of entertainers, musicians, and athletes belonging to Freemasonry is impressive. The fraternity members range from Oscar-winning actors and composers to baseball legends—and all have left their mark on American culture.

A WINNING ROLE IN THE SCOTTISH RITE

The Oscar-winning actor Ernest Borgnine, best known for his role in *McHale's Navy*, is a well-known Mason. He continues to serve as honorary chairman of a program that supports a Scottish Rite Childhood Center.

THAT'S (ENLIGHTENED) ENTERTAINMENT!

It's not surprising that the Freemasons, who look to the wisdom of the ancient Greeks, Romans, and Egyptians for inspiration, value achievement in the arts and athletics as much as these civilizations once did. One Mason in particular served both the Brotherhood and the world with class and stellar humor. A fifty-year Mason, Mel Blanc graced the world with cartoon character voices that only a legend could create. The voice of Bugs Bunny, Porky Pig, and Daffy Duck, among hundreds of others, was a true talent among men. In his distinguished company are other amazing brothers, including magician Harry Houdini, who wowed the world with his astounding feats of escapism, and legendary silent screen swashbuckler Douglas Fairbanks.

Many actors over the years have been Masons, including Gene Autry, Arthur Godfrey, Clark Gable, Tom Mix, Telly Savalas, and Will Rogers. A number of comedians also took their place in the Brotherhood, among them, Bob Hope, Red Skelton, and Oliver Hardy. Even the entire Ringling Brothers circus family—seven brothers and their father—were Masons.

Other entertaining Masons include:

- Edgar Buchanan, former dentist and actor best known for playing Uncle Joe in the classic television series *Petticoat Junction*
- Cecil B. DeMille, legendary film director of such classics as *The Ten Commandments* and *The Greatest Show on Earth*
- Burl Ives, revered singer and actor whose legendary voice can still be heard each Christmas season through the narration of *Rudolph the Red Nosed Reindeer*
- Al Jolson, singer and actor who made history in 1927 acting in *The Jazz Singer*, the first talking picture
- Michael Richards, actor best known for his role as Kramer on *Seinfeld*
- Roy Rogers, actor and legendary cowboy
- Danny Thomas, the actor and philanthropist who in 1962 founded St. Jude's Children's Hospital
- John Wayne, actor and Hollywood legend
- Florenz Ziegfeld, founder of the Ziegfeld Follies

THE TEMPLES ARE ALIVE WITH THE SOUND OF MUSIC

Freemason Duke Ellington was considered to be one of the greatest composers of the twentieth century. His contributions to the music world as a jazz composer, bandleader, pianist, and orchestrator are legendary. Joining him in the Brotherhood is Irving Berlin, himself an exemplary songwriter and musical comedy genius best known for "White Christmas," "God Bless America," and "Alexander's Ragtime Band." Some other Masonic musicians include:

- Eddie Arnold, country music star internationally famous for his rendition of "Make the World Go Away"
- William "Count" Basie, legendary jazz pianist, organist, and orchestra leader
- Roy Clark, singer and country-western star famous for hosting the television show *Hee Haw*
- Nat King Cole, singer and jazz musician
- John Philip Sousa, composer and former leader of the United States Marine Band
- Mel Tillis, country-western singer, songwriter, and actor

GAMES OF THE GODS

Several remarkable athletes have served the Brotherhood with distinction, two of them legendary boxers. Professional Irish-American boxer Jack Dempsey had an exciting career during the early 1900s, as he eventually became a five-time heavyweight champion. His most famous bouts were with Gene Tunney. During World War II, Dempsey became a commissioned officer in the United States Coast Guard. Modern-day boxer and Freemason Sugar Ray Robinson was a six-time world champion in two weight classes. He is considered by many to be the best fighter of all time pound-for-pound.

One Mason in particular has been quite successful in the sport of golf. In the 1950s and 1960s, golf was not a major television event, but Arnold Palmer changed that. His charisma and tournament success led golf pros from America to the British Open and elevated the sport to new heights in popularity.

Ty Cobb and Cy Young, both Masons, secured their legacy in the game of baseball. Cobb was the first player ever elected to the National Baseball Hall of Fame. Young, arguably one of the greatest pitchers the game has ever produced, pitched for more than two decades and earned additional distinction by pitching the first perfect game in modern-day history. "The Flying Dutchman," also known as John "Honus" Wagner, was a Mason and was considered to be the greatest shortstop in the game's history.

FREEMASONRY = FREETHINKING

Freemasons have a long history of thinking outside the box, which is why they've suffered condemnation from so many quarters—from popes to princes. Yet writers, artists, philanthropists, and a wide range of innovative and free-thinking individuals have always taken part in the fraternal order—and continue to do so. Writer and humorist Samuel Clemens, popularly known as Mark Twain, was a Mason, as was writer Alex Haley, author of the groundbreaking novel *Roots*.

THE FIRST BOY SCOUT

Another Mason of particular interest is author and illustrator Daniel Carter Beard, who founded the Society of the Sons of Daniel Boone in 1905. Five years later his group became the first organization of Boy Scouts in America.

At one time considered to be the richest man in the United States, Freemason and German immigrant John Jacob Astor served as Master of New York's Holland Lodge No. 8. He later acted as Grand Treasurer of the Grand Lodge of New

York. If the Astor name sounds familiar, it is because Astor's grandson, John Jacob IV, was lost in the sinking of *RMS Titanic*.

THE MASON WHO BUILT MOUNT RUSHMORE

One Mason who achieved great heights was Gutzon Borglum, a Freemason and sculptor who carved one of the most significant American monuments. Driven to create a fantastic and enormous portrayal of American nationalism, Borglum began carving Mt. Rushmore in 1927 with the help of more than 400 sculptors. It was finished by his son Lincoln in 1941. An astounding feat of masonry, Mt. Rushmore features the faces of Presidents Washington, Jefferson, Lincoln, and Theodore Roosevelt—two of whom were Freemasons.

Other innovative Masons of note include:

- Ezra Ames, prolific eighteenth-century portrait painter who created more than 450 works
- Brad Anderson, famed cartoonist and creator of the comic strip *Marmaduke*
- Robert E. Baylor, cofounder of Baylor University in Texas
- Reverend Norman Vincent Peale, Protestant clergyman known for his groundbreaking book *The Power of Positive Thinking*
- Booker T. Washington, former slave and renowned educator who founded the Tuskegee Institute in 1881

American Freemasons Who Made Their Own History

Perhaps the best part of historical documentation are those pinnacle moments when astounding goals, feats, and personal journeys have been realized. In the past, much about the planet and its inhabitants was unknown, and the thrill of discovery was epic. As the modern age progresses, landmarks of history are often more about acts of self-discovery.

No matter the era, a host of Freemasons have, without a doubt, traveled an historic path, whether they were exploring the great unknown areas of the planet or the untapped resources of human interaction.

Adventures in Freemasonry

Freemasons have negotiated their way through all types of terrain, from the Great Plains to the frigid Arctic, and their adventures have left an indelible mark on history. Even today, it's hard to conceive just how difficult their tasks were and the strength and perseverance required in achieving what many thought was impossible.

MASONS AND THE MORMONS

Joseph Smith, founder of Mormonism and the Mormon Church, and Brigham Young, for whom the famous Utah university was named, were both Freemasons. Both Mormonism and Freemasonry share a penchant for secret rituals performed in temples, among other traditions.

THE LEWIS AND CLARK MASONIC TRAIL

Captain Meriwether Lewis and Second Lieutenant William Clark were both legendary frontiersmen, explorers, and Freemasons. Together in 1804, they embarked on their journey west and didn't stop until they reached the Pacific Ocean. Clark, the mapmaker of the duo, later served as governor of the Missouri Territory. Lewis, in addition to being named a national hero, became governor of the Louisiana Territory. He was also the first Master of a Masonic lodge in St. Louis.

THE KIOWAN FREEMASON

Dr. Parker Paul McKenzie was a Freemason and a Kiowa Indian. When he passed away in 1999 he was the oldest living Kiowa, but that was not his only distinction. During his lifetime, he developed a written language for the Kiowa by creating an alphabet and then recording the words, grammar, and syntax.

FREEMASON FRONTIERSMEN

Christopher "Kit" Carson and Davy Crockett were, in addition to being frontiersmen, part of the Brotherhood, as was William "Buffalo Bill" Cody. Renowned for being a scout and guide, Cody is perhaps best known for founding the Wild West Show, and for Cody, Wyoming, the city named in his honor.

THE MIDNIGHT RIDE OF A MASON

Immortalized as an American patriot is silversmith, engraver, and Mason Paul Revere, who during the American Revolution made his historic midnight ride to Lexington and Concord. It was April 18, 1775, and the warning he and two others delivered enabled American Minutemen to hold back British troops. Revere's alleged shout of "The British are coming!" and his courageous ride were indelibly recorded in a poem by Henry Wadsworth Longfellow.

THE MASONS CLAIM THE NORTH POLE

Yet another famous duo conquered the great unknown, only theirs was a journey of a much different variety. In 1909, Mason and explorer Rear Admiral Robert E. Peary made the amazing journey to the North Pole, becoming arguably the first man ever to do so. It was an astounding accomplishment, one that most individuals felt was an impossible goal. One of Peary's companions on the trek was fellow Mason Matthew Henson, and together they made history.

THE FIRST ARCTIC PHOTOGRAPHER

Another polar explorer was Anthony Fiala, a former cartoonist and Spanish-American War correspondent who, as photographer on a 1901 expedition to the North Pole, took the first moving pictures of the Arctic region. In 1903, Fiala led his own expedition and succeeded in mapping various Arctic islands.

Respite Among the Brotherhood

From epic moments in history to personal claims to fame, Masons have been driven to serve the self-betterment of the planet and its inhabitants. In some cases, Freemasonry served as a conduit for a better life, in others it showed that when individuals are presented with a challenge and are forced to overcome adversity, they rise to the occasion.

The name Robert Pershing Wadlow may not be instantly recognizable, but his participation in Masonry is well known. Wadlow's claim to fame is the fact that at almost nine feet in height, he was the tallest human being on record. Wadlow was accepted into the Masonic youth group, the Order of DeMolay, and eventually became an officer. It is said that the fraternity offered him acceptance, a welcome respite from the rest of the world, which at times was less than kind in regard to Wadlow's astounding height. He passed away in 1940 at age twenty-two.

Charles Stratton, better known as General Tom Thumb, was a Mason of the smallest order. An entertainer and circus performer for P. T. Barnum, Stratton stopped growing at three feet four inches.

FROM SEA TO SHINING SEA

As head of the Central Pacific Railroad, the company responsible for building the first transcontinental line over the Sierra Nevada mountain range, Mason Leland Stanford made history on May 10, 1869, when he hammered in the famous golden spike signifying the final connection of the railways from east and west. He later went on to serve as governor of California and founded Stanford University.

And the Beat Goes On . . .

The list of American Freemasons of note goes on and on. The name James Hoban may not be recognizable, but his work was vital in the building of America's capital city. Hoban, a Mason and architect, designed and oversaw the construction and later renovation of the White House in Washington, D.C. The Irish-born American was also one of the supervising architects of the Capitol building.

Other historic Masons of distinction include:

- Francis Bellamy, the Baptist minister who in 1892 penned the original Pledge of Allegiance
- Stephen F. Austin, considered to be the Father of Texas (the city of Austin is named in his honor)
- Rufus Easton, the first postmaster west of the Mississippi River

- Francis Scott Key, writer of the lyrics for "The Star Spangled Banner"
- Frank S. Land, founder of the Order of De Molay

Conclusion

As this fascinating and impressive accounting of American Freemasons shows, the Brotherhood has left its mark on our country, from Colonial days to the present. It is easy to see why some believe that the Freemasons rule the world—or at least our part of it.

In the next chapter, we'll explore the truth behind the infamous Masonic veil of secrecy—and separate fact from fiction.

CHAPTER 7

THE SECRET AMERICAN HANDSHAKE: FREEMASONS DEMYSTIFIED

There are many mysteries associated with secret societies, and Freemasonry is no exception to the rule. Of course, with mystery inevitably comes misconception and radical opinions based on theories ranging from mild to outrageous. While it is true that Masons do hold secret some aspects of the Craft, it is also true that their secrecy has more to do with privacy. Regardless, like any membership-driven organization, they have certain terms, symbols, and rituals that require explanation in context to the historic fraternal order.

Secret Society or Society of Secrets?

Anti-Masons have dredged up heaps of strident criticism out of the "secret society" moniker that continues to cling to Freemasonry. The very idea of a group of people who exchange ritual greetings, shake hands in a socially recognizable fashion, and hold gatherings in private behind closed doors has been menacingly magical for centuries.

Over those centuries, opinionated, and often exploitive, individuals and groups would have everyone believe that there is something going on in there. In simplistic terms, these criticisms could also apply to board meetings, business conventions, pre-game football meetings, and quilting bees. So, what's with all the secrecy? Much of it lies in history and tradition. Even more of it is misconstrued and misdirected.

Secret Passwords and Handshakes

In the Middle Ages, when operative stonemasons came together to form guilds, there were many professional imperatives for establishing who was and who was not a qualified tradesman. Password greetings and specific handshakes identified craftsmen to one another, and to master masons who could employ them—in much the same fashion a union card serves in modern society. Semiskilled workers who knew just enough about the trade to be dangerous could be identified and either filtered out of the workforce or patiently trained to a journeyman level of ability.

THE SIGN OF THE BROTHERHOOD

From the perspective of safety in an inherently dangerous profession, and to prevent costly errors, there is no question that it served the best interests of journeyman-level masons to keep the identifying signs of their craft jealously guarded.

SOS FREEMASON

Aside from providing employment opportunities, membership in Freemasonry also provided a form of social care and welfare. Masons in dire economic straits could apply for charity, and the families of deceased Masons could receive financial assistance. The temptation to cash in on these opportunities by non-Masons was obvious, and there was a practical necessity of verifying that applicants for charity were true members of the Craft. Record keeping was primitive at best, and the surest way of identifying a needy member of the Brotherhood was by testing his knowledge of closely guarded signals.

REVENGE OF THE TYRANTS

Adolf Hitler blamed the Freemasons and the Jews for Germany's involvement in both world wars. Benito Mussolini dissolved Italian Masonry in 1925, and Spanish dictator General Francisco Franco issued a decree in 1940 that suppressed Communism and Freemasonry.

In such climates, the maintenance of guarded identifying signals and words was an absolute necessity in order to protect one's life, property, and the safety of fellow members. It is worth mentioning that repression of Freemasonry, and of most other forms of free thinking, continues in a number of countries today, including China, Vietnam, and Cuba.

SAFE TRAVELS

Masonic lodges have traditionally greeted roaming members of the fraternity with warmth and enthusiasm. While modern Masonic decorum suggests that traveling Freemasons instigate visits to lodges outside of their jurisdictions through prior contact and letters of introduction prepared by lodge secretaries, Masons in the past were free to visit lodges in other states, provinces, and countries at will. Here again, the knowledge of guarded passwords, hand signals, and Masonic ritual ensured host lodges that their hospitality was being extended to fellow brothers.

PERSECUTED BY SUSPICIOUS MINDS

There have also been strong reasons for guarding the secrets of Masonic membership. Those reasons were triggered by a number of repressive and fanatical regimes throughout history that actively sought out and persecuted Freemasons. Some aristocracies and dictatorships thrived on restricting freedom of thought, and demanded absolute obedience to their authority. As a result, the Masons, a fraternity based on equality, freedom of worship, the pursuit of knowledge and self-awareness, and altruistic charity, ironically found itself the target of suspicion.

SECRETS EXPOSED

Virtually all of the "secrets" of Freemasonry have been revealed at one point or another in history. Exposés have been published from the 1700s to the present day, each promising to reveal more than the last. The Internet is full of sites dedicated to further exposing the so-called secret nature of Masonry. This has done very little practical harm to the fellowship of Freemasonry, and to the contrary, much of the publicity has actually proved to promote and illuminate the philosophies and intentions of the Freemasons.

In the Western world, Freemasons make no secret of their affiliation with the fraternity. Masonic lodges are listed in telephone books and on the Internet, and their activities are publicized and actively promoted. Many Masonic lodges are "pillars" of their communities, and reflect amazing architectural and building expertise. Masonic pins, rings, tie clasps, and paraphernalia are freely available on websites and in stores worldwide. Freemasons are a highly visible force in their respective jurisdictions, and are invariably proud of their association with the fellowship.

SECRETS KEPT

The tradition of guarding handshakes, passwords, and signals of the degrees of Freemasonry continues to this day. Is this necessary in modern society? Probably not. But it does continue a long tradition of quickly identifying other Freemasons, and of maintaining a sense of camaraderie and fellowship. Realistically, it is about as harmful and secretive as the tradition of placing various symbols and graphic images on doors that identify restrooms.

SO MOTE IT BE

One of the most widely used Masonic phrases is "So mote it be," which is spoken at the beginning and end of every lodge meeting. Derived from the Anglo-Saxon word *motan*, it means "to be allowed," or "so may it be." It can also mean "so be it," or when used in prayer, in deference to God, as in "the will of God will be done." Even legendary English poet Geoffrey Chaucer used the phrase in his work to say, "So may it be." In its most simplistic definition in the Brotherhood, it is basically used as an ancient form of the word *amen*, a word that throughout the ages has been used, revered, and respected in its many spiritual incarnations.

To Masons, the phrase "so mote it be" is particularly significant, since these are the final words that appear on the Regius poem, or Halliwell Manuscript. One of the most important documents of Freemasonry, it dates back to the late fourteenth century and includes, among other things, the legend of York and ancient governmental regulations of the Craft.

The Secret Language of Freemasons

Like many organizations, the Freemasons have certain terms and phrases that have specific meaning to the Brotherhood. Many of the terms are based in antiquity and are specific to the Masons as they appear in their tenets, constitutions, rituals, meetings, and legends. Others are general terms that are commonly used in public, such as "third degree" and "on the level."

As most sports have words that are particular to game play, Masons have their own phraseology.

TERMS OF THE TRADE

Many terms that are used by Masons are not necessarily exclusive to the Brotherhood, since they are often used by the general public. The phrase "on the level" or "meeting on the level" indicates that when Masons meet, they meet as equals of all measure. The level by its very nature suggests balance, and for the brethren that translates to equality in regard to each individual's rights, duties, and privileges.

BLACKBALLED

The term "black ball," which is often used to signify someone of fallen reputation or one who has been excluded, applies to the Masonic voting process. Black and white balls are used for voting. If a potential member is "blackballed," meaning he received enough negative votes (literally black balls), it indicates that his membership into the Brotherhood has been denied.

THE SACRED AND THE PROFANE

Anti-Masons are usually quick to misconstrue literal meanings of archaic terms used in Freemasonry. In this instance, the word *profane* bears explanation, because Masonic use of the word is sometime seen as offensive when used in reference to non-Masons.

THE WORSHIPFUL MASTER

Freemasonry is often said to be a religion, which is not the case. Masons do believe in deity, but the Brotherhood itself is not a religious organization. However, several of the titles bestowed upon individuals who hold positions in the Craft and the various rites and degrees individuals earn do contain religious legends, symbolism, and terms like *worshipful* and *priest*. This is often a source of confusion to non-Masons.

OUTSIDE THE TEMPLE

In the ancient form of the word *profane*, the Latin *pro* (meaning "before") and *fanum* (meaning "temple") translates to "outside the temple." It is basically an antonym for the word *sacred*.

When a Mason refers to an individual as *profane*, or to a group of individuals as *profanes*, he simply means that those individuals are not Masons. That distinction means they are not allowed inside a Masonic Temple. It's a matter of semantics and interpretation, and in reality simply indicates nonmembers. Along the same lines, if Masons use the term "profane language," it is meant to indicate words that are not to be spoken within the sanctity of a temple. Perhaps part of the confusion is that the word *profane* is typically linked to *profanity*, which suggests vulgarity.

In Blue Lodge, or Craft Masonry, the individual who is elected leader of a lodge is called the Worshipful Master. ("Blue Lodge" refers to lodges conferring the first three degrees of Masonry.) The term *worshipful*, while religious in connotation, is a title of respect that is not exclusive to Masonry, but is used much in the same way one would use the term *honorable* to address the mayor of a city.

HIGH PRIESTS OF THE ROYAL ARCHES

Degrees relating to the Royal Arch of the York Rite have several ecclesiastical titles, including High Priest, who is the presiding officer of the American Royal Arch Chapter. Contrary to popular belief, a Mason who is serving as High Priest in a Royal Arch Chapter is not a man of the clergy. In reality, the title is more akin to his being a chairman or president of an organization. (In other countries, the term *King* is sometimes used or even *first, second,* and *third Principal.*) This continues in the hierarchy of the Royal Arch with the Grand High Priest and the General Grand High Priest. There is also an Excellent High Priest, Illustrious Master of a Council, and even Eminent Commander of the Commandery, though Masonry has no military force.

The Legacy of Secrecy

Much has been made in the anti-Masonic and conspiratorial worlds about Freemasons instituting secret passwords and handshakes. Taken out of context, a gesture, grip, or odd word spells doom for a society termed "secret." Of course, how secret can it be if everyone knows about it?

Freemasons take an oath that requires them to keep certain things secret, such as the various metaphors of Masonry and certain modes of recognition. Much like any other group or individual, there are certain personal incidents that one means to keep private. It is a matter of semantics, with privacy often misconstrued to mean secrecy. For example, if an individual is denied membership to any organization, the reasons are typically withheld so as to avoid hurt feelings. The same goes for Masonry.

The handshakes and passwords Masons vow to keep secret are minor in the scheme of the world. Critics have in previous centuries charged that these modes of recognition were a form of cronyism; Masons who were looking for work could be given preferential treatment if their employer was a Mason and they recognized one another by a word or gesture. In truth, Masons keep these modes of recognition to themselves out of respect for the Craft and as a show of true fraternal bonding.

THE MASONIC CODEBOOKS

In ancient Masonry, most everything about the Craft—including its rituals and legends—was communicated orally. There are no codebooks in the literal sense, but there are ciphers, which by definition are secretly coded messages. Masons used ciphers as hints to elicit memory of a certain legend or rite.

Sacred Geometry

The art and science of geometry is highly revered in Freemasonry and is one of the most common symbols. As noted, the letter G, which alternately stands for God or geometry, is often used in conjunction with the square and compass (see Chapter 4). Geometry is often said to be the most important of the Seven Liberal Arts and Sciences. In antiquity its links to ancient masons and their trade is obvious: the principles contained in geometry work hand in hand with construction and architecture.

Masonic symbolism, legends, rites, and rituals are replete with geometry. Squares, circles, triangles, angles, and tools used to create geometrical figures are heavily associated with the Craft. They are also most widely recognized by the public. In ancient texts and constitutions Freemasonry is often called geometry, connecting the science and art to the Brotherhood in relation to the very similar principles they share. *Geometry* literally means the "measurement of earth or land," and one can correlate that brothers in much the same way seek to measure their own spiritual and educational progress.

THE DIVINE PRINCIPLE OF AXIOMATIC GEOMETRY

There are two legendary individuals who play a strong role in geometry and in the Craft: Euclid and Pythagoras. Euclid, a Greek mathematician who is known as the "father of geometry," lived in Alexandria, Egypt, until his death in 325 BCE. The author of a series of thirteen textbooks called *Elements*, Euclid used integers and geometrical objects as a base for axiomatic methods, which evolved into modern-day mathematics.

In ancient Egypt there was a marriage of religion and science, taking into account all of the varied gods and their combined knowledge attained in mathematics, geometry, physics, and astronomy. In ancient times, science such as mathematics was considered sacred. The elegant lines and correlations of geometry provided harmony between art and science and the entire world. This further accounts for why geometry is very closely linked to Freemasonry in both its symbolic simplicity and complexity.

The forty-seventh problem of Euclid, also known as the Pythagorean Theorem, is one of the symbolic jewels of a Past Master (a degree in the York Rite). The problem, which was first published by Euclid but discovered much earlier by Pythagoras, is also prominently featured in the initiation and ritual of the third-degree Master Mason. Symbolically, the problem teaches a love of the arts and sciences.

The Knowledge Seekers

Like Euclid, Pythagoras has also had an impact on the Brotherhood. A Greek mathematician and philosopher of the sixth century BCE, Pythagoras is considered to be the "father of numbers." He believed that all things were in relation to mathematics and could be predicted using rhythmic patterns (see Chapter 2).

In 529 BCE, Pythagoras instituted a school at Crotona in Southern Italy that focused on Pythagorean teachings. Many of the school's disciplines were adopted by Freemasons millennia later. A seeker of knowledge and lover of wisdom, Pythagoras clearly had an impact on the educational and philosophical aspects of the Craft.

THE MAGIC NUMBERS OF FREEMASONRY

Numbers, particularly 3 and 7, play a significant part in the fascinating legends of the Craft and in the allegorical lessons taught to the brethren. These numbers are used as memory association tools and learning techniques; certain numbers are connected with specific sets of ideas and legends.

Critics of Freemasonry have had a veritable field day with fanciful attempts at applying numerology to Masonry. Numerology by definition is the study of occult meanings of numbers, but there is nothing remotely occult or secretive in the numbers and their meanings as they are recognized by Freemasons.

THE NUMBER 3

The number 3 carries a staggering volume of references within Freemasonry. There are three degrees of Craft Masonry, three positions of the square and compass, three lighted Cardinal points, three sides to a perfect triangle, the three principle tenets of Freemasonry—the list goes on and on. Lest we forget, there are also the three theological virtues of the Craft—faith, hope, and charity—and the three tenets of brotherly love, relief, and truth.

THE NUMBER 7

As Masonic historians claim, there are hundreds of references to the number 7 in Freemasonry. The construction of Solomon's Temple took seven years; there are seven Liberal Arts and Sciences; Noah had seven days in which to build the ark before the flood came; the ark came to rest on Mount Ararat in the seventh month; the Pythagorean square has four sides and the triangle has three, totaling seven. Again, the list goes on and on.

CONSPIRACY BY THE NUMBERS

The deliberate combination of numbers and ideas in Freemasonry, while undeniably an effective memory and teaching tool, has also provided a great deal of fodder for conspiracy theorists and critics of Freemasonry. It really doesn't take much imagination to fiddle with number combinations that appear to take on the dimensions of a pattern, particularly when that pattern suits the agenda of the number fiddler.

Virtually anyone with a modicum of mathematical ability, a handheld calculator, and an agenda can juggle numbers into a frightening portent of doom and gloom. A few of the more common examples (along with a few of the patently ridiculous) are included here.

THE MARK OF THE BEAST

Freemasonry has been linked to the concept of world domination for years, and because of a single misconstrued reference to Lucifer by Albert Pike, the Brotherhood is characterized as dealing with the devil. In *Morals and Dogma*, Pike wrote: "Lucifer, the Son of Morning! Is it he who bears the Light, and with its splendors and intolerable blinds feeble, sensual, or selfish Souls? Doubt it not." Detractor of Masonry used this as evidence that Pike was a worshiper of Satan.

666

The number 666 is directly referred to in the Bible, in Revelation 13:18, as the mark of the beast, generally known as the anti-Christ, who it is prophesied will bring the world to ruin.

Believers in this conspiracy theory are of the opinion that the Freemasons not only wish to achieve world domination by secretly running the U.S. government, but that they also consort with Satan. These individuals find what they deem numerical proof of this conspiracy in Washington, D.C.

Within the geography of Washington lie Dupont Circle, Scott Circle, and Logan Circle. All of these streets have six major streets running into them, which some believe is a code for the number 666. The House of the Temple, which is the Supreme Council of the Southern Jurisdiction of the Scottish Rite, is bordered by R Street. The letter *R* is the eighteenth letter of the alphabet, and if you add six together three times you get eighteen. This theory persists among some conspiracists despite the fact that the physical address of the House of the Temple is on Sixteenth Street.

UNLUCKY NUMBER THIRTEEN

Other than the demise of Jacques de Molay on October 13, 1307 (Friday the Thirteenth), there is no other meaningful relationship to this number and Freemasonry. Conspiracists have attempted to link Friday the Thirteenth with the Freemason world domination/Satanism theory by pointing out that the American flag has a significant thirteen stripes. These individuals have even gone so far as to claim that the fifty stars are in fact fifty pentagrams.

GET A CLUE!

From the beginning of time, certain geometric shapes have resonated with humans, which accounts for their wide use in architecture and art. The circle, the square, and the triangle are all geometric shapes that man imbued with meaning.

The Circle: In early cultures it represented divine male energy, which was why halos were round. Because a circle also has no beginning and no end, it came to represent infinity, perfection, and eternity, which is why it often symbolized God.

The Square: To the Hindus, squares represented order in the universe and the balance of opposites. Its symmetry and solidity also came to represent an earthy dependability.

The Triangle: With its three points, a triangle represents the trinity—the divinity of three. Trinities exist in many religions: Christianity's Father, Son, and Holy Spirit; Judaic Kabbalism's Kether, Chokmah, and Binah; ancient Egypt's Osiris, Isis, and Horus; Hinduism's Brahma, Vishnu, and Shiva. If the triangle points upward, it represents ascension to heaven—the fire in man to ascend; if the triangle points downward, it represents a graceful descent from heaven, or a more passive, feminine energy.

Concentric Circles: These are a symbol of the cosmos.

The Crescent: A crescent represents the newly born, the ability to change shape, and the ability to carry man from darkness to light. When paired with a star, it represents sovereignty and divinity.

The Hexagram: In the Kabbalistic tradition, the six-pointed star comprised of two overlapping triangles symbolized the six directions of space, the union between male and female divine energy, and the four elements of earth, wind, fire, and water. In alchemy, the triangles represent the fire and water elements, and the combination represents perfect harmony. The hexagram symbol was frequently used alongside the pentagram in antiquity and they are thus interlinked.

The Pentagram: An endless line (like the circle), the pentagram represents perfection and wholeness. Its triangles represent the four elements, plus spirituality, which endows it with the power to subdue and destroy evil. «

TILL DEATH DO US PART

For as long as organized Freemasonry has existed, so have anti-Masons and other sundry theorists who've criticized the Brotherhood for the practices and rituals it performs under an alleged blanket of secrecy. Critics often cite Masonry for what it terms their "blood oaths," which critics deem both archaic and offensive. To Masons, the oaths are entirely symbolic in relation to ancient legend, and there is certainly no actual blood involved in any rituals. The oaths taken by the brethren are serious to them, and refer only to penalties in regard to each individual's obligation to the Brotherhood. In the most simplistic form, the oaths represent a man's shame in breaking a promise.

BLOOD OATHS

Much of the hysteria of the past and present regarding blood oaths likely stem from the Legend of Hiram Abiff, which figures prominently in rituals and initiation ceremonies of Craft Masonry (see Chapter 4). In order to comprehend the symbolism of the alleged blood oaths, it is important to understand that part of the legend in context.

THE ORIGIN OF BLOOD OATHS

The penalties to which blood oaths refer originated in Medieval England's legal system. At one time these were real punishments that were carried out on individuals who opposed religious or political tyranny.

According to legend, when King Solomon became aware of the plot to murder Hiram, he sent searchers in an attempt to find him. It was one of those searchers who heard the lamentations of the three perpetrators as a result of the heinous act they'd committed. First heard was Jubela, who cried:

"O that my throat had been cut across, my tongue torn out, and my body buried in the rough sands of the sea, at low water mark, where the tide ebbs and flows twice in twenty-four hours, ere I had been accessory to the death of so good a man as our Grand Master, Hiram Abiff!"

Jubelo was the next to be heard:

"O that my left breast had been torn open and my heart and vitals taken from thence and thrown over my left shoulder, carried into the valley of Jehosaphat, and there to become a prey to the wild beasts of the field and vultures of the air, ere I had conspired the death of so good a man as our Grand Master, Hiram Abiff!"

And then Jubelum, who confessed:

"O that my body had been severed in two in the midst, and divided to the north and south, my bowels burnt to ashes in the center, and the ashes scattered by the four winds of heaven, that there might not the least track or remembrance remain among men, or Masons, of so vile and perjured a wretch as I am; ah, Jubela and Jubelo, it was I that struck him harder than you both. It was I that gave him the fatal blow; it was I that killed him outright."

After being returned to face King Solomon, the three men professed their wishes to die, and they were executed in the manner each described. Jubela's throat was slashed, his tongue torn out, and his body buried in the sand. Jubelo's heart was removed and his innards tossed over his left shoulder for the vultures to devour, and Jubelum was cut in half, his parts carried in separate directions, and his bowels burnt to ash.

When swearing a blood oath during the initiation ceremony, candidates repeat the words supposedly spoken by Hiram Abiff's murderers all those centuries ago.

JACK THE RIPPER: THE CELLULOID FREEMASON

In the movie *From Hell*, which follows the so-called royal conspiracy theory that Jack the Ripper was a Freemason, two of the Ripper's victims had their hearts removed and their vitals tossed over their right shoulders.

DEATH BY SYMBOL

When reading of the murder of Hiram Abiff, it's easy to see how one could misconstrue the term "blood oath" in relation to Masonic ritual. When the initiate repeats the words spoken by the three ruffians, it is purely symbolic. While it is true that Masons do take their obligations seriously and that there should be some penalty for dispensing confidential information, it is in no way literal. In Freemasonry there are only three actual penalties—reprimand, suspension of membership, or expulsion—for violating laws of the Craft. No one has ever been harmed during initiation proceedings or as a result of leaving the Brotherhood.

Conclusion: The Secrecy Continues

The Freemasons' insistence on secrecy may have been breeched over the years, but still the Brotherhood is one based on confidentiality, loyalty, and mystery. This is not bound to change, now or in the future.

In the next chapter, we'll examine some of the symbolism and allegory that veil the Freemasons' most closely guarded secrets.

CHAPTER 8
THE SECRET SYMBOLS OF AMERICA

The Masonic Brotherhood is rich with symbolism that is at the same time historic and highly allegorical in nature. Many Masonic symbols have a host of interpretations associated with them, but in general many of the objects are in direct relation to operative Masonry (from the days when Masons were primarily carpenters) and the tools of the trade. Symbols are often characterized as drawings, shapes, colors, letters, or objects that represent something in particular. In Masonry, symbols run the gamut from actual tools and architectural details to religious and geometrical philosophies.

The Signs Are Everywhere
Most people have seen a number of Masonic symbols in architecture, literature, and cinema, most likely without realizing they are symbols of the Craft. The square and compass are often deemed the most significant symbols of Freemasonry and are widely recognized. The all-seeing eye that graces American currency is highly visible and a source of eternal debate. Lesser known are the symbolic beehives, pillars, and lambskin aprons.

Symbols associated with the Craft are taken very seriously, as evidenced by their importance in various Masonic initiation rites and public ceremonies such as burials. When used in conjunction with the Volume of Sacred Law, the square and compass become highly significant, as they form the Three Great Lights of Masonry. The combined moral square, the virtuous compass, and the sacred volume as a conduit to God become a formidable and powerful symbol.

FREEMASONRY SQUARED

The square is one of the Three Great Lights of Masonry and a working tool for Fellowcraft Masons. It also serves as the official emblem of the Master Mason.

The conceptual triad of body, mind, and soul also relates to the Three Great Lights and the three-tiered structure of Masonry. The square as body, the compass as mind, and the Volume of Sacred Law as soul reinforces the symbolic nature of earth, heaven, and man's relation to deity.

Many Masonic symbols are evolved from ancient practices, each bearing its own interpretation and associated allegory—be it of a practical, spiritual, physical, or religious nature. The point within a circle, for example, has many varied representations derived from ancient times. Pillars, dating back to the time of Solomon's Temple, provide plenty of speculation from architectural to the obvious phallic symbolism.

Tools of the Trade

Operative Masons made use of a wide variety of tools, each unique in their perfection, design, and purpose. Many of these tools, like the square, compass, plumb line, and level, relate to geometry. Other tools, like the trowel, gavel, and apron, are more practical. A variety of esoteric symbols, such as the hourglass, scythe, and pot of incense, are also prevalent within the Craft.

GET A CLUE!

Among the most secret and important ancient symbols is the "Hand of the Mysteries." This object can be fashioned from stone, wood, or even sketched. It shows a hand with three of the fingers clasped in a fist, and the thumb and index finger pointing toward something. A crown is tattooed on the thumb and a star on the index finger. These tattoos are part of the symbolic invitation to action, as are the tattoos on the other three fingers: a sun, a lantern, and a key.

In ancient times, the Hand of the Mysteries was a highly treasured invitation to pass through a portal or gateway to join a sacred, secret society whose purpose was to guard the ancient wisdom of the ages. The Hand of the Mysteries earmarked its recipient to acquire secret knowledge. The hand is typically presented in a sacred space and provides directions to a temple, the name of the master who will teach you, or a clue to what comes next on your path to enlightenment. «

One example of a symbolic and ancient masonry tool now used in speculative Freemasonry is the trowel, one of the working tools of the Master Mason. In practice the trowel is used to spread cement, the binding agent that glues all parts of a structure together. As a symbol this represents the spreading of kindness and affection that unites brethren the world over.

The gauge and the common gavel are also familiar symbols of the Brotherhood carried over from ancient times. The twenty-four-inch gauge, or rule, was used by masons to lay out their stonework, and has become a symbol representing all types of measure, both in the literal and figurative sense. The number 24 applies to the size of stones being cut and also to the number of hours in a day. Masons are taught to divide a full day into thirds, with eight hours devoted to the service of God and the relief of others in distress, another third for one's work, and the last portion for rest.

ORDER IN THE TEMPLE!

The gavel symbolically given to the Master Mason is called Hiram, in homage to the Hiram Abiff, the architect of Solomon's Temple. Like Hiram, this gavel governs the Brotherhood and instills order in the lodge.

The common gavel, one of the working tools of the Entered Apprentice, was a tool used to break off corners of a squared block of building stone called *rough ashlar*. Symbolically, it encourages individuals to rid themselves of the vices and impurities of life, preserve a positive disposition, and fit the body as a "living" stone for the spiritual temple.

SQUARE AND COMPASS

Though simple in its nature, the square is one of the most significant symbols in Freemasonry, one that retains many historic and allegorical meanings. The square symbolizes earth, and it also represents morality and truthfulness. To act honestly is to act "on the square." To the operative Mason, the square has a plain surface and sides angled at ninety degrees, and its purpose is to test the sides of a stone for accuracy.

Historically, the square is highly revered in many ancient cultures and retains specific meaning. Squares often symbolize perfection and goodness. Egyptian architects used a perfect square as the base for their pyramids. Chinese cultures believed the square represented goodness and just behavior. It is said that there is nothing more true than a perfect square—its sides equal to one another and its angles sharp.

The compass, unlike the familiar magnetic directional compass used by mariners or aviators, is a V-shaped measuring device used by operative Masons to determine the proportions of all aspects of a building's design. Architects use the compass to ensure the stability, accuracy, and beauty of their designs. Like the square, the compass is one of the most important and prominent symbols of Freemasonry. It is meant to symbolize virtue as a measure of one's life and conduct, and it also signifies restraint, skill, and knowledge.

Used in tandem, the square and compass are the most visible symbols of Freemasonry, ones that have appeared throughout history—especially ancient carvings and works of art—and are often prevalent in modern-day art, literature, and film. A common interpretation of the square and compass is that it represents the union of heaven and earth: the square symbolizes earth, and the compass, the arc of heaven.

SIGNS OF THE RIPPER

In the 2001 film *From Hell,* starring Johnny Depp, the square and compass are prominently featured on Jack the Ripper's case of surgical instruments.

The heaven and earth symbolism is related to astronomy. In his study of the stars, ancient man quickly realized that the square was not well suited for analysis of the heavens, but a circle would prove invaluable, especially in determining specific points. The compass was ideal for astronomical measurement and a natural companion to the earthbound square. In time, the compass and its circular renderings came to symbolize the spiritual virtue of man. A circle without end signified eternity and the Divine, and gave reason for man to gaze upward and pay homage to the Supreme Being.

PLUMB AND LEVEL

Both the plumb and the level were tools used by operative Masons to prove that surfaces were horizontally level or perfectly upright. The Latin word for lead is *plumbum*. A plumb line is a cord or line that has a lead ball attached to the bottom. With this, the mason can use gravity to his advantage and test vertical walls to ensure his work is upright. Symbolically this extends to a man in that he will stand straight—like a solid wall—and not crumble under strain or pressure. The plumb line represents uprightness and rectitude.

The level by its very nature is symbolic of spiritual balance and equality. For Masons it is a measure of balance, especially on a horizontal plane, and for the operative Mason, this was crucial in the laying of stone. For all things to be equal, everything must be level. It is a similar concept to the plumb line in regard to perfection and symmetry, only it relates to horizontal measure. In Masonry, the level represents equality and the balance of the brethren, with each brother issued equal rights, duties, and privileges.

The Wearing of the Apron

At first glance it might be odd to think of men who aren't chefs walking around in white aprons, but the symbolic apron contains a rich history. In speculative Masonry, its importance is immediately obvious to the Entered Apprentice, and it increases in significance when a brother rises to Master Mason. The apron is, in fact, the dress code of the brethren, as everyone in attendance at lodge gatherings is required to wear his apron.

THE APRON THROUGHOUT HISTORY

The apron as a symbol has appeared in many cultures and sects throughout history. Some speculate that Adam and Eve originated the apron when they fashioned aprons out of leaves after their notorious fall from grace. The apron has symbolized truth, pride, honor, preference, and in the case of royalty, it signified authority. Aprons appear in ancient Egyptian imagery, as well as Greek, Roman, and Palestinian depictions, and in the Jewish religious sect of Essenes from the second century BCE. Even Israelite clergy wore ephods, a type of girdle with an apron down the front.

Aprons used by Masons in the Middle Ages were typically made of animal skin and were quite large. They were held by a leather strap around the neck, tied around the waist, and covered the mason from his chest to his ankles. Knee-length versions were later introduced, but it is speculated that leather aprons such as these were worn by many stonemasons until the early 1800s.

THE FIRST MASONIC APRON

According to some historians, the earliest representations depicting a Masonic apron appear in 1717 in an engraved portrait of Grand Master Anthony Sayer, and in 1723 in an illustration on Anderson's *The Constitutions of Free-Masons.*

The practice of decorating aprons was begun sometime around the 1730s, as Masonic symbols became decorative additives. This artistic convention is now part of the blue lodge degree ceremonies.

APRONS IN RITUAL

The apron is considered to be the badge of a Mason and one that is evident at each lodge meeting. In the first degree a newly initiated Entered Apprentice receives a pure white lambskin apron as his "badge of innocence." Now his permanent property, the apron is void of decoration, which serves to remind him of the purity of life and rectitude of conduct necessary for his ascension. Over time, brothers may receive different types of aprons, but for the new brother this first apron is highly significant because it denotes his admission into a lodge and his first gift given to him by the lodge.

The significance of the lambskin is twofold. Lambs by their very nature have historically symbolized innocence and slaughter. Innocence to the Apprentice represents his birth into the Craft. The esoteric aspect of his innocence indicates that he is free of moral defect.

A MASON OF TRUE GRIT

In a scene from the 1969 Western *True Grit*, starring John Wayne, Kim Darby's character views her deceased father in the funeral parlor and then tells her farmhand, "When you get home, you put him in a better coffin and you bury him in a Mason's apron."

Individuals awarded a Fellowcraft degree also receive a white lambskin apron, but theirs features a pair of sky-blue rosettes at the bottom. The apron of the Master Mason, which represents a position of authority, expands in decoration with the addition of a sky-blue edging and lining, and another rosette on either the fall or flap of the apron. Only officers or past lodge officers have aprons adorned with their official emblem, typically in white or silver and featured at the center of the apron.

The Letter G

As mentioned, the letter G is another greatly revered and highly visible symbol of Freemasonry. It's no secret that God and geometry are deeply embedded in the Craft, and as such, both share in the representation of the letter G. Reference to God as the Grand Architect of the Universe or Grand Master of the Universe is also a common interpretation. Where the symbol originated remains unclear, and it should be said that the letter G most often appears in regard to American and Canadian Masonry but less frequently in Britain and European brethren.

THE G RING

One of the most sacred symbols of the Craft, the letter G in North American Masonry is often placed in the center of emblems such as the square and compass. It's also very common on Masonic rings and other jewelry.

GET A CLUE!

A Masonic ring typically has an ornate seal featuring a two-headed phoenix and the number 33 emblazoned above it. Thirty-three represents the highest degree of Masonry. If the member achieves Worshipful Master status, his ring will have a small "33" symbol on the band. In the past, Worshipful Masters were responsible for protecting the mysteries and would often dip their rings in hot wax to seal packages containing secret information. «

The marriage of geometry and Freemasonry has been a long and prosperous one, as ancient masonry is intrinsically linked to architecture, which involves geometrical aspects. Many experts have surmised that the letter G shows no strict evolution as a Masonic symbol; however, it is a commonly held belief that the

G originally stood for *geometry* and slowly grew to represent God when the second, or Fellowcraft, degree was established in the eighteenth century. During the Fellowcraft initiation rite, a candidate is first introduced to the Seven Liberal Arts and Sciences, which includes geometry.

RISING FROM THE FLAMES

The phoenix has been used as an emblem by many cultures and countries from the time of antiquity. With its promise of rising from the ashes, it symbolizes immortality and resurrection or rebirth—themes echoed in the ancient rituals in which initiates acquired wisdom and were then symbolically reborn. The motif was prominent in ancient cultures, such as China (whose version derived from the Egyptians), Greece, and the American Indians (whose thunderbird was very similar to Greece's phoenix). It also came to represent the human quest of universal good—of man serving mankind.

As a representation of God, the letter G serves as a reminder that all individual actions are seen by God, that deity pervades nature and all men, and that life's blessings, which emanate from God, are disrupted when a man's actions are contrary to "Divine Will." The G in relation to deity is no stranger to antiquity. In the Greek alphabet it is the letter *Tau*, and in Hebrew it is *Yod*.

The aspects of God and geometry give the letter G a powerful place in Masonic symbolism. Brothers of the Craft regard the universe as one of the grandest symbols; together with the aspect of deity and the science of geometry, a deep bond is formed. In a sense, they give an individual the virtue needed to build a temple of divine thoughts for his soul.

GET A CLUE!

When Masons meditate, they may use the following symbolic items to assist their process.

- **Skull:** Man's transformation through decay, a reminder that we all shed our mortal flesh
- **Sulpher:** Alchemical catalyst that facilitates transformation
- **Salt:** Alchemical catalyst that facilitates transformation
- **Hourglass:** Transformational power of time
- **Unlit candle:** Formative primordial fire and awakening of man from his ignorant slumber, transformation through illumination
- **Giant scythe:** The transformative power of nature, the reaping of nature's gifts «

Other Significant Masonic Symbols

As a Brother progresses through the degrees of the Craft, he is taught the deeper meanings of Masonic symbols, which through the use of allegory serve to further enhance his education and spirituality. Many of these icons are common to ancient civilizations, and they are open to a wide range of interpretation. Symbols often relate to science, architecture, and theology or the spiritual ascension of mankind, while those of an esoteric nature, like the scythe and hourglass, represent life and time.

TRACING BOARDS

In simple terms, a tracing board is the more primitive equivalent of a PowerPoint presentation that highlights various pictures and symbolism. During the early days of speculative Masonry, symbols were drawn on the floor in chalk, which could later be washed away. Eventually the system evolved into drawing images on floor cloths that could then be rolled up and reused. The floor cloths were eventually placed on easels, and by the eighteenth century they were transferred to tracing boards.

CLIMBING THE MASONIC LADDER

The ladder is another common Masonic symbol that inherently represents advancement and ascension from a lower to a higher plane. Ladders have historically been used as symbols in many cultures and typically have seven rungs.

Tracing boards are commonly used as a training tool during various degree initiation rites, and they contain pictures and emblems specific to each degree. The drawings shown on the boards are highly symbolic and rich in allegory and are meant to confer a sense of history to the initiate and his brethren. Tracing boards are often confused with trestle boards, which were used by operative Masons to place building designs and blueprints.

Pillars

In the Craft, pillars encompass several different symbolic systems and ideologies. Pillars are, of course, deeply rooted in history, as evidenced by most ancient civilizations. Greek, Roman, and Egyptian architecture features pillars with various designs and emblems, while at the same time these pillars serve as monuments for various religious and symbolic beliefs.

The pillars on the porch and their symbolism play a large role in the initiation ceremony of the Fellowcraft degree, but the allegory surrounding these two pillars is prevalent throughout the Craft. In the Bible the pillars are named Jachin and Boaz, and they stood at the entrance to the Temple of Solomon. A striking presence, they represent establishment and strength and by association further the concept that a man must have a balance of power and control in his life in order to find ultimate success. It is speculated that globes atop the columns alternately represent the celestial (heaven) and terrestrial (earth) respectively

Symbolically, Masonic lodges are supported by three great pillars denoting wisdom, strength, and beauty. The pillars further allude to the lodge's three principal officers. The pillar of wisdom is the Worshipful Master, who as the lodge's teacher can offer instruction and fraternal stability. The Senior Warden is the pillar of strength, who assists the Master in lodge details and supports the harmony of the brethren. The pillar of beauty is the Junior Warden, whose observance of the sun maintains the beauty of the day.

PILLARS OF MASONIC STRENGTH

According to some historians, the two pillars of Solomon's Temple symbolize the Pillar of Cloud and Pillar of Fire that guided the Israelites to the Promised Land.

Vertical Lines and the Point Within a Circle

The point within a circle and the two vertical lines associated with it are symbols of Freemasonry that are open to many different interpretations, some practical and some esoteric. In some instances, for example, a closed circle with a point in the center is representative of deity and man's relationship to God. In general, however, it's fair to say that these two symbols are geometric in origin. The point is simply a dot surrounded by a circle, and the vertical lines appear on either side of the circle in parallel formation.

One common interpretation relates Freemasonry's patron saints, St. John the Baptist and St. John the Evangelist, to the calendar and two days that mark extreme seasonal shifts. It is said that John the Baptist represents summer solstice and John the Evangelist, winter solstice. In this instance, each is a vertical line on either side of an allegorical sun, which rotates between them. In this interpretation the symbols represent control of one's conduct. Taking it one step further, it is also said that in this speculation, the two vertical lines refer to the zodiac signs of Cancer and Capricorn.

CIRCLES OF GOLD

Alchemy by definition is a process of transmutation through means of a seemingly magical power. In regard to that science, the point within the circle symbolizes the sun and philosophic gold.

Another theory about the symbols relates back to the circumambulation that takes place during a degree initiation ceremony. The circle represents the circuit that an initiate makes around the lodge's altar, which represents the point within the circle. Brethren standing on either side of the altar are then symbolic of the vertical lines.

Still another allegorical connection dates back to ancient mystical times and the symbolism of the phallus as male regeneration. In megalithic sites such as Stonehenge, single stones were often erected in the center of circles. As a representation of virility it becomes almost a religious symbol, which in some cultures points to sun worship and the regenerative powers of the sun.

Beehives

At first glance, a beehive might seem an unusual symbol to associate with a secret society, but in truth it's highly emblematic. The beehive signifies industry, not in the traditional modern-day sense of manufacturing, but as devotion to a specific task or endeavor. Masonic definitions of the beehive imply that all individuals are born into the world as rational and intelligent beings and, as such, should be industrious and never be content to not offer aid to others if it is in their power to do so.

GET A CLUE

In ancient Egypt, the symbol of a dot inside a circle was the symbol for Ra, the sun god. Modern astronomy uses it to this day as a symbol of the solar system. Eastern philosophy uses it to symbolize the third eye; Kabbalists use it to symbolize Kether, the highest Sephiroth and the most hidden of all things; early mystics called it "the Eye of God." Pythagoreans used it as a symbol of Monad, the Divine Truth, the Prisca Sapientia, the at-one-ment of mind and soul. In *The Lost Symbol* it is the inspiration for the "all-seeing eye" on the Great Seal. It was also an ancient symbol for gold.«

Industry is a virtue that is taught to all Masons, in particular the Master Mason. The wages each Mason earns to support his family can also be used to help another brother or that brother's family if they are in distress. The bee and hive analogies mirror that cause. Alone a bee can do very little, but once the bee is in the hive and part of a systemized industry, it becomes infinitely easier to accomplish singular tasks or goals.

Volume of the Sacred Law

The most prominent of the Three Great Lights of Masonry (the square and compass being the other two) is the Volume of the Sacred Law. It must be said that the oft-used term *bible* is a misnomer. Because members of the Craft practice many different religions, the sacred text of choice varies. For Christian Masons, it is indeed the Holy Bible; however, as mentioned, during degree ceremonies initiates are allowed to choose which sacred text they wish to be laid upon the altar.

The Volume of the Sacred Law is crucial to the perfection of a lodge, as its teachings help rule and govern individual faith. No individual can become a member of the brethren without professing belief in the grand truths contained within the sacred text he has chosen. The Sacred Law represents truth, which, when combined with the square (morality) and compass (virtue), represents the search for ultimate truth within the sacred text.

THE ROYAL BUZZ

Many ancient and modern cultures held the bee in high regard. For the Egyptians, bees signified obedience and worship of a remarkable king. After his coronation, Napoleon adopted the bee as a symbol that stood for efficiency and productivity and also as an emblem of immortality and resurrection. Bees were also heraldic symbols of the Barberini family in Rome during the Renaissance—a powerful clan that produced three popes.

The Anchor and the Ark

A pair of highly significant symbols are the anchor and the ark, which represent hope and a well-spent life. The anchor is a hope of glory and fulfillment of God's promises to the soul, a symbol of keeping steadfast to faith despite temptation. The ark refers to the Ark of the Covenant, the sacred chest said to contain the Ten Commandments.

In Masonry terms, the anchor and the ark together signify a divine ship that carries Masons over a sea of troubles to a safe harbor where they can drop anchor.

Esoteric Symbols

There are a number of esoteric symbols denoting different aspects of the Craft, several of which apply to the degree of

Master Mason. The pot of incense is emblematic of purity of heart and is a symbolic sacrifice to deity. The glowing heat of the incense mirrors the glow of gratitude in one's heart toward the author of existence and the blessings one enjoys.

The hourglass and the scythe allegorically represent time in regard to the human journey. As a measuring device, the hourglass contains a fixed amount of sand that descends from the top to the bottom chamber in the span of an hour. As a Masonic symbol, it represents human life for the fact that we cannot comprehend the tiny particles that imperceptibly pass until at last the hour ends. Life is short, but it should never be wasted, and when the end arrives, death escorts us to a dark resting place.

The scythe, a long, curved, single-edge blade, cuts through the brittle thread of life and launches us into eternity. If we escape the evils of early life and eventually reach old age, we are cut down by the scythe of time and sent to the land of our forefathers.

Conclusion: Symbols of the Ages

As we've seen in this chapter, the symbols used in Freemasonry are derived from the Ancient Mysteries—and their hidden meanings are clues to the rituals and practices of the Craft. In Part Three, we'll explore the many people and places, art and architecture, institutions and organizations that make up Secret America—and the ways in which all Americans can share in our esoteric heritage.

AMERICA THE MYSTERIOUS

America has her secrets, but most of them are obscured, not hidden. All around us in our art, our architecture, and our culture are the clues to our past, present, and future—if only we know how and where to look. In Part Three, we examine and deconstruct the surprising esoteric symbolism of our most familiar objects d'art, landmarks, and monuments, and delve into the secret societies that are most active in our nation today. We also acknowledge the burgeoning field of modern-day noetic science, and unveil the ways in which today's scientists and symbologists are claiming the Ancient Mysteries as their own, thus setting the stage for an enlightened America—from sea to shining sea.

CHAPTER 9

THE SECRET ART AND ARCHITECTURE OF AMERICA

From the Pyramids to the Parthenon, Michelangelo to Dürer, the Capitol to Mount Rushmore, art and architecture have always reflected the secret desires, dreams, and dogma of the society in which they are created. As we'll see in this chapter, nothing is as it seems—and even the most recognizable sculpture, painting, or building is a veritable hotbed of clues waiting to be deciphered.

George Is God: The Apotheosis of George Washington

The Apotheosis of Washington, the famous 4,644-square-foot fresco by Constantino Brumidi, is often called "the Michelangelo of the Capitol" because it covers the canopy of the Capitol Rotunda and represents the transformation of man into God. Specifically, the painting shows George Washington being transformed into a god.

Brumidi, who completed some of his finest work at the Vatican in Rome, immigrated to America in 1852 to work on the U.S. Capitol. In the central panel, Washington is depicted ascending in white robes, accompanied by thirteen maidens. Nearby, Minerva is presenting technological inspiration to our nation's great inventors: Benjamin Franklin, Robert Fulton, and Samuel Morse. Vulcan is present to assist in building the steam engine; Neptune is illustrating how to lay the transatlantic cable; Ceres is resting on the McCormick reaper. These images reflect the fact that our forefathers believed they were being offered great wisdom from the gods—to perform godlike tasks.

In his novel *The Lost Symbol,* Dan Brown says that the Capitol Rotunda once housed a massive sculpture of a bare-chested Washington, sculpted in 1840 by Horatio Greenough. The statue rested in the same position as Zeus in the Pantheon, left hand holding a sword, right hand raised with thumb and finger extended. Once banished to a shed in the east garden, it now resides in the Smithsonian's National Museum of American History. (Brown is almost right—the statue of Zeus was from the temple at Olympia, though it doesn't exist anymore and we must rely on ancient accounts to deduce what it must have looked like.) Today, few people realize that the statue of Washington offers some of the last vestigial links to a time when the father of the country had watched over the Capitol as a god.

THE AHA! MOMENT: APOTHEOSIS

Most religions or belief systems promise a coming age of enlightenment in which the apotheosis of man will occur (man will become one with God). This collective belief has various names:

- Hindus = Krita Age
- Astrologers = Age of Aquarius
- Jews = Coming of the Messiah
- Theosophists = New Age
- Cosmologists = Harmonic Convergence
- Mayans = December 21, 2012

Emblem of the Gods: The Great Seal of the United States

No symbol of our nation reflects the influence of the Ancient Mysteries or its devotees more than the Great Seal of the United States. Designed by our forefathers, this seal has been used to verify the authenticity of federal documents since the earliest days of our government. It reflects our Founding Fathers' fascination with and admiration for the wisdom of the Ancients. This same fascination and admiration proved the battleground for conflicting views over which symbols, images, and language should appear on the final seal. Three committees involving fourteen men debated symbolism for half a dozen years before a final design was approved by Congress in 1782.

Designed by Committee: The Great Seal

On July 4, 1776, Congress commissioned Thomas Jefferson, Ben Franklin, and John Adams to design our fledgling nation's first pendant seal—a two-sided seal with an observe (front) and a reverse (back). Portrait artist Pierre Eugène Du Simitière collaborated and executed their designs for presentation to Congress.

Although some assume that Franklin and Jefferson were strongly influenced by their familiarity with Freemasonry and thus incorporated esoteric imagery, in fact, the designs submitted by Franklin and Jefferson as part of this first committee were based on biblical imagery. John Adams suggested a mythological image based on Hercules. In fact, the only person whose ideas actually made it to the final design was Du Simitière. His contributions consisted of the following:

- *E Pluribus Unum*
- A shield

- MDCCLXXVI
- The all-seeing-eye of Providence in a triangle with a glory or rays of light emanating from the eye

THE SECOND COMMITTEE

In 1777, Congress rejected the ideas of the first committee but waited three years before forming a second committee. This committee consisted of John Morin Scott, James Lovell, and William Churchill, all three of whom had served in the Continental Congress. The artist on this committee, Frances Hopkinson, had also served in the Continental Congress and had been one of the signers of the Declaration of Independence. He was a Freemason and had helped design the American flag that was accepted by Congress in 1777, which may be why his ideas took precedence. Hopkinson suggested the following:

- Red and white stripes on a blue background for the shield
- A radiant constellation of thirteen stars
- An olive branch

Congress again rejected the designs, and formed a third committee in 1782.

THE THIRD COMMITTEE

This committee consisted of Arthur Middleton, John Rutledge, and Elias Boudinot. Middleton, who had also served in Congress and had signed the Declaration of Independence, ended up playing a minor role, and Rutledge opted out altogether and was replaced by Arthur Lee. Boudinot, who had also served in Congress, as its president, teamed up with Lee and Charles Thomson, Secretary of Congress at the time, to hire William Barton as the artist/consultant. Barton's contributions were, as follows:

- An eagle for the obverse (front)
- An unfinished pyramid for the reverse (back)

Finally, in 1782, Thomson and Barton created the design that was approved for the Great Seal.

THE ADEPT-TATION OF ROBERT LANGDON

In ancient times, the Adepts recorded the Ancient Mysteries in codes, employing a metaphorical language of symbols, myth, and allegory to prevent this esoteric wisdom from falling into the wrong hands. According to *The Lost Symbol*, these encrypted symbols are widely visible in our art, our architecture, and our literature. What we have lost is the ability to decode them. Robert Langdon, the protagonist in the novel, seeks a secret magical password to unlock the Ancient Mysteries. This word, or *verbum significatium*, is buried underground, waiting for its moment in time to be unveiled. Supposedly its unlocking can only occur when mankind can no longer survive with the wisdom of the ages and its unveiling will usher in an apotheosis or new age of enlightenment.

Birds of a Democratic Feather

During the debate over the seal, the various committees considered a number of motifs involving birds. Many of the designs submitted for consideration featured a bird strongly resembling a phoenix on its nest of flames as the central motif—representing a rise from the ashes and rebirth. Ben Franklin loved the idea of the indigenous wild turkey as the chosen symbol, noting that it represented the spirit of citizens: hardworking, industrious, and morally virtuous. When asked about an eagle, Franklin nixed the idea, noting that an eagle was a bird of prey with few admirable qualities.

THE PHOENIX: REAL OR MYTHOLOGICAL?

Early writers such as Clement, Herodotus, and Pliny all described the phoenix bird, noting its glossy purple feathers, blue and red tail plumes, light-colored head that bore a circle of gold plumage, and a tuft of brilliantly colored feathers lifting from the back of its head. Other than these descriptions, we have no proof that an actual phoenix existed, although it is said that it once lived in distant parts of Arabia.

THE BALD EAGLE HAS LANDED

The original drawing for the seal done by William Barton featured a phoenix and an eagle. In 1782, when Congress asked Charles Thompson to revise the design, he insisted on a bald eagle rising. He also elected to have the eagle's claws grasp a bundle of arrows in one talon and an olive branch in the other.

The symbols on the final seal include:

- A shielded bald eagle soaring upward, with wings aloft
- A banner above the eagle's head reading "*e pluribus unum*" (Latin for "out of many one")
- Thirteen stars above the banner
- A bunch of arrows that are grasped tightly in one of the eagle's talons and an olive branch in the other

THE PYRAMID OF THIRTEEN

For the back of the seal, Benjamin Franklin proffered the image of Moses parting the Red Sea, while Thomas Jefferson suggested the leaders of the Anglo-Saxon invasion of Britain. Ultimately the Pyramid of Giza was the icon that graced the Great Seal. Pyramids have been symbols of resurrection, rebirth, and even reincarnation since the time of the ancient Egyptian Pharaohs who built them. They also represent the Ancient Mysteries—the timeless wisdom that survives all generations of man.

— GET A CLUE! —

The phoenix, half eagle and half pheasant, represents man's immortality: his ability to rise from his ashes, to resurrect again and again. In ancient lore, a phoenix lived for 500 years and then new life emerged from its center. Hence the connection to rebirth or rising from the ashes. It also represents the new life that can come from acquiring wisdom. As noted above, the traditional symbol of the highest degree of masonry, the thirty-third degree, which is awarded to the Worshipful Master of a Masonic lodge, contains an embossed seal with a double-headed phoenix with the number 33 scripted above. «

Ancient Egyptians believed that the Pyramid of Giza was the enshrined tomb of the god Thoth (Hermes to the Greeks), the personification of personal wisdom. No trace of the usual capstone has been found at Giza; rather, it was topped with a platform. Some believe that the pyramid was left unfinished to represent the idea that humans and human societies are a work in progress. The pyramid itself has been considered an image of the universal house, and its floating "all-seeing-eye" was interpreted as a radiant symbol of the Great Architect of the Universe bestowing spiritual radiance or enlightenment.

FROM ATLANTIS TO ANCIENT EGYPT TO AMERICA

The legendary American adept Edgar Cayce based his belief that Hermes/Thoth was an engineer from the submerged Atlantis on information gleaned during his psychic trances. Cayce believed that Hermes/Thoth designed and directed the construction of the Pyramids of Egypt.

13 X 72 = FREEMASONRY

The Pyramid of Giza as rendered on the Great Seal is composed of thirteen rows of seventy-two stones each—without a capstone. The "all-seeing eye" floats above the tip of the pyramid with rays of sunlight bursting forth from it. While some complained that the illustration was nothing more than a boring version of a Masonic emblem, given the significance Freemasons among other seekers of divine truth placed on numbers, that was probably considered a good thing by our Founding Fathers. At any rate, they approved this image, and to this day it graces not only the Great Seal but the U.S. dollar bill as well.

THE "OFFICIAL" SYMBOLISM OF THE GREAT SEAL

Charles Thompson provided the following explanation of the Great Seal's symbolism when he submitted the design to Congress for approval.

The Escutcheon is composed of the chief & pale, the two most honorable ordinaries. The Pieces represent the several states all joined in one solid compact entire, supporting a Chief, which unites the whole & represents Congress. The Motto alludes to this union. The pales in the arms are kept closely united by the chief and the Chief depends upon that union & the strength resulting from it for its support, to denote the Confederacy of the United States of America & the preservation of their union through Congress.

THE KABBALAH OF THE GREAT SEAL

The four-letter word for God, YHWH, that appears in the Hebrew bible is known as the Tetragrammaton, usually rendered in English as *Jehovah* or *Yaweh*. In the Middle Ages, Kabbalists discovered that this name could be combined in seventy-two forms, creating what was called the Shemhamforash and representing the laws, powers, and energies of nature necessary for the ascension or perfection of man. On the Great Seal, the seventy-two stones of the pyramid are symbolic of the Shehemforash.

The colours of the pales are those used in the flag of the United States of America; White signifies purity and innocence, Red, hardiness & valor, and Blue, the colour of the Chief signifies vigilance, perseverance & justice. The Olive branch and arrows denote the power of peace & war which is exclusively vested in Congress. The Constellation denotes a new State taking its place and rank among other sovereign powers. The Escutcheon is born on the breast of an American Eagle without any other supporters to denote that the United States of America ought to rely on their own Virtue.

Reverse. The pyramid signifies Strength and Duration: The Eye over it & the Motto allude to the many signal interpositions of providence in favour of the American cause. The date underneath is that of the Declaration of Independence and the words under it signify the beginning of the new American Æra, which commences from that date.

THE GREAT PYRAMID OF ACCOMPLISHMENT: AMERICA

"Most of the patriots who achieved American independence belonged to these societies, and derived their inspiration, courage, and high purpose from the ancient teaching. There can be no question that the Great Seal was directly inspired by these orders of the human Quest, and that it set forth the purpose for this nation as that purpose was seen and known to the Founding Fathers."

—Manly P. Hall, *The Secret Destiny of America*

Hall is one of many who believe that the combination of phoenix, pyramid, and "all-seeing-eye" was not coincidental, but rather the intentional choice to use symbols meaningful to various secret societies that existed in the new nation before the Revolutionary War.

The Great Seal recognizes, in the minds of the Founding Fathers and members of those secret societies, America as the "new Atlantis," a continent in which a great pyramid of accomplishment would arise, a nation blessed by the Great Architect or God, a nation dedicated to the fulfillment of the Divine Will—achievable as long as its citizens and leaders remained dedicated to the principles inherent in our unique destiny.

Bald Eagle Art in the Capitol

In addition to its position on the Great Seal, the bald eagle is a ubiquitous symbol in our nation's Capitol as well. Benjamin Latrobe, one of the architects working on the design of the

Capitol Building, either sketched or had someone else sketch an eagle for an entablature for the Capitol building. Giuseppe Franzoni, an Italian sculptor hired to create sculptures for the Capitol, thought the design was too tame to be such an important symbol of America.

FREEDOM FEATHERS

Atop the Capitol dome, Thomas Crawford's famous statue of Freedom's helmet has a headdress of eagle feathers. For years many observers assumed it was a Native American headdress.

Latrobe then requested that his friend Charles Willson Peale send him drawings of the head and claws of a bald eagle. Peale not only provided the requested art (executed by his artistic sons) but sent Latrobe a real stuffed head and claws from his museum's bald eagle collection.

When the British set the Capitol aflame in 1812, the original Franzoni sculpture of the bald eagle was destroyed. Today, only sketches of it exist. By 1816, Giuseppe Valaperta had sculpted the one that today graces the great chamber of the Capitol.

Other eagles in the Capitol:

- Masonic architect Charles Bullfinch had Luigi Persico sculpt an eagle that was placed alongside his sculpture of the Genius of America, which rests over the central portico.
- Architect Thomas Walter had an eagle placed immediately below the bust of Columbus when they cast what are now known as the "Columbus doors" that lead into the central portico.

David Ovason, author of *The Secret Architecture of Our Nation's Capital*, calls the "fearsome-looking" bird an "open mystery" (ancients called the eagle "occult blind"), explaining that—like the Masonic and Rosicrucian heraldic birds, and all that preceded them—it was intended to be inspirational to the uninitiated yet also hold secret meaning for the enlightened, those aware of arcane symbolism.

ENTER THE U.S. DOLLAR BILL

The obverse of the Great Seal has been used by the Department of State since 1782, but the public had no idea it existed until 1935 when it was first printed on the 1935A dollar bill. The release of the obverse may not have been premeditated or given any heavy significance, but it did appear at the time when our democracy was struggling with the Depression, in between one World War fought and a second one looming.

National Gallery of Art

In 1937, Congress passed a resolution creating The National Gallery of Art on the basis of a gift from famed financier and Freemason Andrew W. Mellon. Art collected by Mr. Mellon during the 1920s and 1930s formed the foundation of his bequest. Famed architect John Russell Pope, who also designed the Jefferson Memorial, designed the building in the neoclassical style inspired by the Pantheon in Rome. On March 17, 1941, President and fellow Freemason Franklin D. Roosevelt received the gallery and its artwork on behalf of the people of the United States of America.

Today, this spectacular gallery consists of two beautiful structures and houses art by such Renaissance masters as Fra Angelico, Bellini, Botticelli, and Leonardo da Vinci, whose work is rich in symbolism.

ALBERCHT DÜRER: MYSTIC CHRISTIAN ARTIST

The National Gallery of Art also houses the *Melencholia 1*, the famous engraving by Albrecht Dürer in the Rosenwald Collection. According to Dan Brown's *The Lost Symbol*, this painting depicts mankind's struggle to comprehend the Ancient Mysteries. Art critics have often interpreted the engraving as Dürer's depiction of his own tortured state of mind at this point in his career.

Dürer was a sixteenth-century German engraver and painter considered by many to be the ultimate Renaissance man. An artist, philosopher, alchemist, and lifelong student of the Ancient Mysteries, he practiced Mystic Christianity, a fusion of early Christianity, alchemy, astrology, and science. Among his works are:

- *Adam and Eve*
- *The Betrayal of Christ*
- *The Four Horsemen of the Apocalypse*
- *The Great Passion*
- *The Last Supper*

As previously noted, Dürer's *Melencholia* includes a magic square that contains the date on which Dürer completed the work. Significantly, the engraving includes many of the tools of architecture, including those symbolic of the Masons. Others have suggested that the engraving also contains alchemical symbolism.

The engraving depicts a brooding figure with giant wings seated in front of a stone building, surrounded by a cacophony of objects that may or may not have any relation to one another: measuring scales, an orb, a polyhedron, an emaciated dog, carpenter's tools, an hourglass, various geometric solids, a hanging bell, a putto (a childlike angel), a blade, a ladder, and so on.

In the most widely accepted interpretation, the winged figure represents human genius in the form of a man who is depressed at his inability to achieve enlightenment. The objects are all strewn around him—objects representative of math, science, philosophy, nature, geometry, and carpentry— all symbolizing his inability to achieve enlightenment despite his intellect.

Melencholia 1 was the first European work of art to feature a magic square. Some historians believe this was the artist's way to send a coded message that the Ancient Mysteries had migrated from Egypt to Europe, where they were guarded by secret societies.

THE ZODIAC FOUNTAIN

The Mellon Memorial Fountain at the National Gallery of Art in Washington, D.C., is also known as the Zodiac Fountain, thanks to the twelve signs of the zodiac that adorn its lower portion. The influence of astrology is evident in art and architecture all over the city, from this magnificent fountain to the equally magnificent 1937 Steuben glass ceiling at the Federal Reserve Board.

ASTROLOGY: A MULTICULTURAL SYMBOLISM

The ancient practice of astrology is a major source of symbolism that seemed to develop independently in different civilizations.

The Chaldeans, who lived in Babylonia (now Iraq), developed astrology as early as 3000 BCE, and the Chinese were practicing astrology by 2000 BCE. Astrology was known in ancient India and by the Maya of Central America. By the sixth century BCE, astrology had spread to Greece, where Pythagoras and Plato used it in their study of religion and astronomy.

It is clear that certain astronomical bodies, particularly the sun, affected the change of seasons and the success of crops. So it's not a big leap to assume that the movements of other bodies such as the planets affected or represented additional aspects of life. They also gave us our notions of time—from the daily cycle of night and day; the lunar cycle of twenty-eight days, which gives the month by subdividing the four phases of the moon; and the yearly cycle of twelve lunar cycles (or about 360 daily cycles).

Twelve is an important number in astrology because twelve complete lunar cycles takes approximately one year. Each month was eventually identified with a sign of the zodiac, which is believed to have originated in Mesopotamia as early as 2000 BCE. The Greeks adopted the symbols from the Babylonians and passed them on to the other ancient civilizations.

The Egyptians assigned other names and symbols to the zodiacal divisions. The Chinese also adopted the twelve-fold division, but called the signs rat, ox, tiger, hare, dragon, serpent, horse, sheep, monkey, hen, dog, and pig. The Aztecs independently devised a similar system. Twelve thus symbolized *a complete cycle*; and twelve was also used to divide the day and the night.

Conclusion: In the Beginning There Were Symbols

The secret art and architecture of America is evident not only in particular works but also in the people and places of our nation. In the next chapter, we'll take a look at secret places in the Mecca of all American symbolism—Washington, D.C.

CHAPTER 10

OUR SECRET CAPITAL: WASHINGTON, D.C.

The federal government tried eight locations before settling on Washington, D.C. In 1785 Congress voted to establish a permanent site for the nation's capital. The northern colonies wanted it to be located on the Delaware River; southern colonies wanted it on the Potomac. Virginia's Thomas Jefferson achieved a compromise when he introduced legislation that mandated that the federal government would pay the Revolutionary War debt of the colonies if New York's Alexander Hamilton and other northern legislators would agree to the southern location. George Washington, who lived nearby at Mount Vernon, selected the diamond-shaped, 100-square-mile plot.

In 1791 Pierre L'Enfant, who had fought in the Revolutionary War, was commissioned to design Washington, D.C. Much of L'Enfant's vision was made reality over the next half century, save for the tree-lined boulevard that he envisioned lined with houses; this instead would eventually become the Mall.

As a man who had trained as a surveyor, George Washington held a vision for the capital, one that included a spectacular site, held meaning, and reflected the providence of his nation's destiny. No one knows if Washington was aware that the final site was in the same vicinity as the place where Algonquin Indians held their tribal grand councils, but we can be fairly certain that he recognized the symmetry of the fact that because of the hills in the region, the area had once been named Rome.

ALL ROADS LEAD TO ROME, USA

In 1663, a man named Francis Pope owned a hill in the region of the Potomac River. According to lore, before he owned the hill Pope had a prophetic dream in which he envisioned a splendid parliament house on its summit. He purchased the land and named the hill Rome, anticipating its future as a great city. He also named the tributary that ran along the property the Tiber. While the story of the prophetic dream might be Pope's fanciful imagination at work, there is a deed recorded in the Maryland State Archives, dated June 5, 1663, that recorded survey information, including the name of a strip of land called Rome and an inlet, the Tiber.

GET A CLUE!

Our forefathers knew well that the plot of land that is now Washington, D.C., had been originally named Rome, and the river that runs through it the Tiber. Loving that symbolism, they erected pantheons and temples adorned with visages of the classical gods and goddesses: Apollo, Minerva, Venus, Helios, Vulcan, Jupiter, and so on.

Standing in the capital's center is the Washington Monument, our own classical Egyptian obelisk, larger than the ones in Cairo or Alexandria. The Capitol Rotunda itself has more than a dozen gods, which is more than the original Pantheon in Rome. In *The Lost Symbol,* Dan Brown says the Rotunda was designed as a tribute to the Temple of Vesta, which was circular with a wide hole in the floor to allow the keepers of the flame (the Vestal Virgins) to tend the sacred fire of enlightenment. He claims, not entirely accurately, that the Capitol Rotunda was designed as a tribute to the Temple of Vesta and once had a wide hole in its floor, one that covers the Capitol Crypt where a fire was kept burning. According to Brown, a female "Keeper of the Crypt," a federal employee, kept the flame burning for fifty years, until the hole was closed.

It's true that there was once a ten-foot-wide hold in the floor of the Rotunda, but its purpose was more mundane than the one Brown assigns it. By 1842 Greenough's statue of George Washington was so much of a laughingstock that a decision was made to move it to the Capitol Crypt beneath the Rotunda. A hole was created in the floor so sightseers could look down on the statue. The hole created drafts and dampness in the Rotunda and was eventually closed.

The Lost Symbol says that a four-pointed compass is embedded one story below the Capitol Rotunda's first floor, covering the site of the eternal flame, a symbol of America's flame that once shed illumination toward the four corners of the world. «

Now let's examine some of the buildings scattered through this new Rome, buildings that embodied both the pride and spirit of the growing nation as well as its secret heritage.

The Capitol Building

The cornerstone for the Capitol Building was laid during the morning of September 18, 1793, when the sun was passing through the twenty-fifth degree of Virgo. This point in the zodiac occurred when the moon would promote the greatest happiness and well-being, which many trace to the Masons' vision of Washington, D.C., as a city destined to become the center of the new world.

GIFTS OF THE GODS

The mural gracing the inside of the Capitol Building's dome depicts the Founding Fathers and other great minds of their age receiving wisdom directly from the Roman gods:

- Ceres sits on a McCormick mechanical reaper, bringing agricultural science to Americans.
- Vulcan forges cannonballs in front of a steam engine.
- Venus helps to lay the transatlantic telegraph cable.
- Minerva is shown bringing an electrical generator, batteries, and a printing press to the great American scientists Benjamin Franklin, Samuel Morse, and Robert Fulton.

National Statuary Hall

The building resembles a Greek amphitheatre, with a balanced semicircle, sandstone walls, breccia columns, and statues of thirty-eight prominent Americans standing in a semicircle on a black-and-white checkerboard marble floor. There are 100 statues in the Hall's collection, but others are placed in various parts of the Capitol and other Washington buildings.

Washington Monument

While most of us grew up thinking the Washington Monument is a uniquely American memorial to our first president, it is, in fact, the world's tallest obelisk at 555 feet. The obelisk has roots dating back to ancient Egypt and Freemasonry and is one of the most prominent, visible symbols of America's mystical background.

In fact, the obelisk is intimately linked with the Egyptian star of Sirius and the god Baal. In sacred hieroglyphics, an obelisk represented the star of Sirius, and altars to Baal often took the form of obelisks.

The monument had been part of the original plan for the city, but it was originally not an obelisk. In 1783, the Continental Congress decided to honor Washington with an equestrian statue. Pierre L'Enfant marked the location with a pyramid of stones, which many believed marked the exact center of the original ten-mile square of the new city, though that turned out not to be true.

After Washington died, the city's planners envisioned a massive tomb and asked Mrs. Washington for permission to move her husband's body from Mount Vernon to the planned tomb. Unfortunately, this did not happen before Mrs. Washington died, which meant they never received permission to move his body.

KING GEORGE, PHARAOH OF THE UNITED STATES

In 1800, the House of Representatives proposed the memorial to Washington should take the form of a pyramid that would be 100-feet wide at the base and proportional in height.

The first design is preserved in the Library of Congress. It involves a gigantic pyramid that would feature the Masonic concept of a human pyramid contained within a greater cosmic pyramid. The hollow interior would have contained a triple-tier room surrounded by four hallways and four corner rotundas. The light would have come from the oculus at the apex.

The Senate rejected the pyramid concept, and progress stalled. The Washington National Monument Society, formed in 1833, sought fresh ideas for a monument. Finally, a new monument was designed by Masonic architect Robert Mills.

Mills turned the pyramid design into an obelisk. His original plans for the monument included a colonnaded rotunda whose entablature would carry statuary of a four-horse chariot, representing the sun god Helios. By plunking Washington into the chariot, many felt the design implied that Washington was a god. At the top, Mills wanted to place a five-pointed star. As the obelisk was being built, however, the military engineer Thomas Lincoln Casey (who also supervised construction of the Library of Congress) decided to honor the original design and add a pyramid at the top. After further delays, the monument, which has in some ways become *the* symbol of the city, was eventually completed in 1884.

OBELISKS OF ORDER

Baal, one of the sons of El, chief god of the Canaanites, was the executive god of the pantheon, the god of thunder and winter storms, the dynamic warrior god who champions the divine order against the menacing forces of chaos. An upright pillar became a symbol of Baal-worship and was also associated with the goddess Ashtoreth, who represented the productive principal of life, sister to Baal's representation of the generative principal. Originally obelisks, constructed from red granite stone were erected in pairs at the entrances to ancient Egyptian temples.

Although the obelisk resembles the "sun images" or altars of Baal, which stood in ancient Babylon and Egypt, it was primarily chosen, it seems, because Freemasons typically erected obelisks at their gravesite. Washington's obelisk stands in perfect line to the intersecting point or the form of the Masonic square, stretching from the House of the Temple—the Supreme Council of the Southern Jurisdiction of the Scottish Rite—to the Capitol.

THE PYRAMIDIC CROWN

While not an actual pyramid, the apex of the Washington Monument is pyramidic in that the engineer in charge, Thomas Casey, narrowed the obelisk to a point. The apex is built up from thirteen layers of stonework, yet it is constructed of aluminum instead of the building blocks of stone or marble that Masons preferred. Some wonder if Casey intended to give the illusion that the pyramid is not officially finished, evoking an image similar to that of the unfinished pyramid on the dollar bill. An earlier design had an apex very similar to the one on the dollar bill, allowing light to enter the darkness of the triangle. Scholars have postulated that this design was scrapped because it was "too Masonic," reflecting their eternal struggles between light and dark, symbolism that remained in the foundation and cornerstone ceremonies by scheduling the events during an astrologically favorable time, as noted previously.

As mentioned by Dan Brown in *The Lost Symbol,* a 3,300-pound capstone sits atop the monument; an 896-step winding, square spiral staircase wraps around an open elevator shaft and descends hundreds of feet beneath the capstone. The zenith of the monument consists of a tiny tip of aluminum, a precious metal at the time and representative of man's enlightened mind, straining toward heaven. The tip is in the shape of a one-foot tall pyramid, and it bears a one-inch-tall inscription that says *Laus Deo* (Latin for "praise God"). Brown's protagonist Robert Langdon suggests to his companion, Katherine Solomon, that it could also be interpreted in light of symbols, as follows:

L = the stonemason's square

AU = the element gold

S = the Greek Sigma

D = the Greek Delta

E = Alchemical mercury

O = The Ouroboros

THE MISSING LINTELS

The surviving prints, drawings, and photographs show that both the east and west doors to the monument once had false lintels or beams over the doors that were decorated with an Egyptian motif: the eagle-like wings of the Horus bird carrying the sun. This was a common design element in Ancient Egypt and almost certainly symbolized fortuitous cosmic blessings. Some speculate that Thomas Casey removed them when the initial W was carved over the sun, implying the George Washington was being deified.

GET A CLUE!

A symbol from ancient Greece and Egypt, the ouroboros depicts a snake swallowing its own tail. The symbol merges the meaning of the circle with the meaning of a snake, as well as other symbols. It denotes the eternity of existence and the unending circle of life, death, and rebirth. «

THE CIRCLES

The location of the monument marks the center of Washington, D.C., the point from which a pattern of streets and monuments radiate outward. Its circular concourse is made of white stone, save for two decorative courses of dark stone that form two concentric circles around the monument. In *The Lost Symbol*, this becomes the "circle with the circle" or the great circumpunct symbol for God, which Robert Langdon suggests means that God is at the heart of our nation.

THE STONES

During construction, the U.S. accepted donated stones from individual states, foreign countries, militia companies, churches, literary groups, and cultural societies, including, of course, Masonic Lodges. As a result, there are a variety of inscriptions and symbols relevant to the donors. Among the oddities is a stone from Wales whose Gaelic inscription proclaims "Our language, our country, our birthplace, Wales forever."

Another strange stone, which Dan Brown brings into the plot for *The Lost Symbol,* is one donated by the Grand Lodge of Maryland in 1850. According to Brown's description in the novel, it's a large stone medallion depicting a cloaked figure holding a scythe, kneeling beside an hourglass. The figure's arm is raised with its index finger pointing toward an open Bible. Note that the scythe, hourglass, and Bible are all Masonic symbols.

This stone has an engraving of a mysterious winged figure with what appears to be fire—or at least a strange lock of hair—emerging from the top of his head. The figure is pointing toward an open book, which may or may not be the Bible. On top of the book, holding down its pages, are Masonic symbols of a square and compass. This stone is one of many donated by the Grand Lodge of Maryland, and because vandalism became a massive problem in previous decades, it is only viewable on ranger-led tours.

THE SMASHING OF THE POPE

In 1851, during construction of the monument, Pope Pius XI offered the U.S. Legation in Rome a block of marble from the Temple of Concord. Because the block of marble was inscribed with the words "Rome to America," a group known as The Know Nothing Party, who were concerned about what they believed was growing Catholic influence in government, was enraged. They believed the proposed gift was a plot by the Vatican, intended to overthrow the country's religious freedom. In March 1854, some masked members of this group stole the block of marble and smashed it, dropping pieces in the Potomac. The Know Nothing Party's adherents also managed to take over for a time the planning and execution of the monument, which led Congress to deny additional funds, grinding construction to a halt.

THE CORNERSTONE

The cornerstone for the Washington Monument, like many of the cornerstones in Washington, D.C., was laid in accordance with Masonic practices—and when astrological conditions were ripe. It appears that an astrological chart that had been prepared indicated that the ideal day for laying the cornerstone occurred in the twenty-fifth degree of Virgo, shortly after the moon progressed into Virgo. Planning the cornerstone's laying for this date was designed to foster happiness and well being for the nation.

CLARA'S CRAWL SPACE

In 1997, a government employee discovered a sealed crawl space above the third floor of 437 7th Street, the former office and residence of Clara Barton, famous Civil War nurse and founder of the American Red Cross. The room contained U.S. Civil War artifacts and documents that had been gathering dust for more than 100 years. The room has been preserved by a women's historical society.

Library of Congress

The Library of Congress was constructed after several fires — one set by the British during the War of 1812 — ravaged the Capitol, destroying historical documents vital to our nation. Considered a symbol of American's thirst for knowledge and belief in the dissemination of knowledge, the Library of Congress is also what many consider the most beautiful building in America. It is also a hub of arcane symbolism. This symbolism may have been well known to General Thomas Lincoln Casey, chief of the Army Corps of Engineers, who was placed in charge of construction of the library's current building in 1888. (As noted, General Casey also oversaw construction of the Washington Monument.) Beginning in 1892, Edward Pearce Casey, the son of General Casey, began to supervise the interior work, including sculptural and painted decoration by more than fifty American artists.

MOVE OVER, ALEXANDRIA

The Library of Congress has become the largest library on earth, housing more than 500 miles of shelves containing books, documents, and artifacts—enough to stretch from Washington, D.C., to Boston. It includes Thomas Jefferson's personal collection of more than 6,000 books on science, philosophy, and even astrology. Jefferson donated this collection to Congress to form the basis of the library and immediately began assembling a second library for himself, purchasing books from Europe and from booksellers throughout the United States.

The library is housed within three buildings in Washington: The Thomas Jefferson Building, the John Adams Building, and the James Madison Memorial Building.

Inside the Thomas Jefferson building, the oldest part of the library, one encounters a wide hallway of Italian marble, stucco, and gold leaf that is lined with statues, all depicting the goddess Minerva. A seventy-five-foot ceiling has magnificent stained glass skylights and paneled beams adorned with aluminum leaf (more rare than gold at the time of construction). Two curving staircases have newel posts supported by giant bronze female figures holding torches of enlightenment. The stairway banisters are carved with cupid-like putti (childlike angels) portrayed as modern scientists.

ADAMS, JEFFERSON, AND MADISON

John Adams and Thomas Jefferson became close friends during the run-up to the Revolution, and their friendship solidified in the years following the American victory at Yorktown. When Jefferson's wife died, Abigail Adams became a nurturing figure to Jefferson's daughters. Adams and Jefferson remained close when both were sent to Europe on diplomatic missions.

At the same time, Jefferson was drawing close to James Madison, who kept Jefferson closely informed of the progress in drawing up a constitution for the young republic.

In the campaign for the election of 1800, Adams and Jefferson were on different sides. The campaign was bitter and hard-fought, and the two became both political and personal enemies. Jefferson won the election to become the third president of the United States, and Adams retired to his estate in Massachusetts.

In 1812 the two men reconciled and began a correspondence that lasted until their deaths, on the same day, July 4, 1826—exactly fifty years after the signing of the Declaration of Independence.

In the center of the floor is the sun, on which are noted the four cardinal points of the compass. These compass points correspond to directions within the library. For example, the Main

Reading Room is to the east. The inlays represent the twelve signs of the zodiac, beginning with Leo in the northwest corner. Proceeding clockwise, the others are Cancer, Gemini, Taurus, Aries, Pisces, Aquarius, Capricorn, Sagittarius, Scorpio, Libra, and Virgo.

To the east, above the second-story pavilion, there are thirty-three heads. Each was sculpted by Otis T. Mason, a curator of the Department of Ethnology at the time, to represent each race in the world—and perhaps the number of degrees available to Masons, as well as the Masonic desire to blend all "good men" into one brotherhood. These heads are arranged so some are facing in each of the four directions.

In the portico, there are nine busts of famous men, three of whom were Masons, facing only to the west. These busts represent literary genius and the magnitude of past achievements.

THE BIBLES IN THE NEW WORLD

The library's two most valuable books—the Giant Bible of Mainz, handwritten in the 1450s, and America's copy of the Gutenberg Bible, one of only three perfect vellum copies in the world—are stored in bulletproof display cases.

The reading room of the library has a voluminous octagon rising 160 feet at its center. The eight sides are finished in chocolate brown Tennessee marble, cream-colored Siena marble, and apple-red Algerian marble. Because it is lit from eight angles, there are no shadows. A golden dome, similar to the Capitol Building's dome, encapsulates the reading room on the exterior, while the interior of the dome is laden with many symbols.

A towering central collar has rays of arabesque coffers curling down the dome to an upper balcony. Encircling the room are sixteen bronze "portrait" statues, and beneath them is a stunning arcade of archways forming a lower balcony. At floor level, three concentric circles of burnished wood desks radiate out from the massive octagonal circulation desk. In *The Lost Symbol*, Dan Brown's protagonist, Robert Langdon, discovers a secret opening in one of the cabinets that leads to the circulation system, which consists of a conveyor system that ferries books via conveyor belts through a web of underground tunnels that link the three buildings that comprise the library.

THE FIVE-POINTED STAR

Atop the columns in the main reading room, amidst the Egyptian-revival carvings, are five-petal tobacco leaves, a distinctly American symbol representing its mercantile system, which some also believe alludes to the Masonic symbol of a five-pointed star, based on an Egyptian hieroglyphic symbol. It also resembles the forget-me-not flower that served as the secret badge of fraternity for Freemasons in Nazi Germany. Today it is the official emblem for Freemasons in Germany.

In *The Lost Symbol*, Brown describes a long tunnel beneath Independence Avenue that links the Library of Congress with the Capitol Building. In fact, the basement of the Capitol Building has so many hidden nooks and crannies that it resembles a labyrinth. Passageways lead to all five office buildings where members of Congress and the Senate have their main offices, as well as to the Library of Congress.

In the John Adams Building, to the east of the Thomas Jefferson Building, the history of the written word is depicted in sculpted figures by Lee Lawrie on the bronze doors at the west (Second Street) and east (Third Street) entrances. The center doors at the west entrance contain six figures, which are repeated on the flanking doors of the east entrance. The figures on the center doors are:

- *Hermes*, the messenger of the gods
- *Odin*, the Viking-Germanic god of war and creator of the runic alphabet
- *Ogma*, the Irish god who invented the Gaelic alphabet
- *Itzama*, god of the Mayans
- *Quetzalcoatl*, god of the Aztecs
- *Sequoyah*, an American Indian

The two flanking doors of the west entrance depict six other figures who represent the history of the written word. The figures, repeated on the center door of the east entrance, are:

- *Thoth*, an Egyptian god
- *Ts'ang Chieh*, the Chinese patron of writing
- *Nabu*, an Akkadian god
- *Brahma*, the Indian god
- *Cadmus*, the Greek sower of dragon's teeth
- *Tahmurath*, a hero of the ancient Persians

WHAT DO THOSE STARS MEAN ON THE SIDE OF GEORGETOWN TOWNHOUSES?

In Georgetown, star emblems on the side of townhouses on the canal aren't some mystical code. They served a utilitarian purpose: they were installed to shore up the houses. Until the mid 1800s, many of the early Georgetown Federal-style townhouses were held together with a cast-iron pole that ran from one wall to another. The poles were fastened on the outside with these cast-iron rods capped with the stars.

National Cathedral

In 1792, Pierre L'Enfant's "Plan of the Federal City" allocated land for construction of a "great church for national purposes," although the National Portrait Gallery now sits on that site. The National Cathedral was constructed on a fifty-seven-acre site on Mount Saint Alban. Frederick Bodley, England's leading Anglican Church architect, served as head architect.

The Cathedral Church of Saint Peter and Saint Paul, better known as the National Cathedral, is an Episcopal Church situated in the center of our nation's capital. As such it has often served as the nation's spiritual heart. The neo-gothic masterpiece, at the north end of Embassy Row, is the sixth-largest cathedral in the world (its highest tower reaching thirty stories high), the second largest in the United States (after the Cathedral of St. John the Divine in New York City), and the fourth tallest building in Washington, D.C.

THE CATHOLIC CHURCH IN WASHINGTON, D.C.

The first house of worship in Washington, D.C., was St. Patrick's, a Catholic church founded in 1794. The cornerstone for the current cathedral was laid in 1872.

To avoid a violation of the First Amendment (which provides for the separation of church and state), the Protestant Episcopal Cathedral Foundation, under the leadership of nine bishops of Washington, erected the cathedral under a charter passed by the United States Congress on January 6, 1893. Construction began in September 1907, when President Theodore Roosevelt laid the cornerstone, and continued, with extended breaks during wartimes, for the next eighty-three years. The foundation continues to own and operate the cathedral, which does not receive federal funding.

Its Gothic architectural features include flying buttresses, pointed arches, ceiling vaulting, more than 200 stained glass windows, carved stone decorations, and three towers. The building consists of a long eight-bay nave with wide side aisles and a five-bay chancel, intersected by a six-bay transept. The south porch has a large portal with a carved tympanum. This portal is approached by the Pilgrim Steps, a long flight of forty-foot-wide steps. The top of the Gloria in Excelsis tower is the highest point in Washington. There is a Pilgrim Observation Gallery halfway up the west-end towers that provide sweeping views of the city.

THE UNITED STATES OF THE CHURCH

The National Cathedral Association (NCA) has more than 14,000 members, more than 88 percent of whom live outside the Washington area. They are divided into committees by state. Every year, a state has a state day at the cathedral, during which that state is recognized by name in the prayers. Every four years, a state has a Major State Day, at which time those who live in the state are encouraged to make a pilgrimage to the cathedral, and dignitaries from the state are invited to speak. American state flags were displayed in the nave until 2007; currently the display of the state flags alternates throughout the year with the display of liturgical banners hung on the pillars, reflecting the seasons of the Church year.

The pulpit was carved out of stones from Canterbury Cathedral; Glastonbury Abbey provided stone for the bishop's cathedral, his formal seat. The high altar, the Jerusalem Altar, is made from stones quarried at Solomon's Quarry near Jerusalem, reputedly where the stones for Solomon's Temple were quarried. In the floor directly in front of that altar are set ten stones from the Chapel of Moses on Mount

Sinai, representing the Ten Commandments, as a foundation for the Jerusalem Altar.

The cathedral also has a stained-glass window called the Space Window because it has a fragment of the moon rock embedded in it, and a statue of Darth Vader, one of the cathedral's more modern grotesques, in the west towers. Darth Vader was a product of a contest for children to design a gargoyle that depicted the face of evil.

SHADOW HOUSE

The Shadow House, referred to as the Carderock Gazebo in *The Lost Symbol*, is located in the medieval-style walled garden just west of Embassy Row. It was designed by cathedral architect Philip Hubert Frohman and constructed between 1927 and 1928. It received its name from a medieval term for *gazebo*, and is made of locally quarried Carderock stone that once was part of President Grover Cleveland's summer home, Red Top.

Frederick Law Olmsted, Jr., the designer of New York's Central Park, and Florence Bratenhal, wife of the second dean of the church, were hired in the early 1900s to design the famed National Cathedral Bishop's Garden where the gazebo is located. Olmsted designed the Pilgrim Road winding up Mt. St. Alban from Garfield Street, the South Road to Bethlehem Chapel where the nave foundation was being laid, and the Bishop's House (now known as the Church House) garden with its surrounding walls and lawn, which included herb, rose, and perennial beds.

Folger Shakespeare Library

The Folger Shakespeare Library, founded by oil tycoon Henry Clay Folger, is a major center for scholarly research. It houses the world's largest collection of Shakespeare's printed works, as well as other rare Renaissance books and manuscripts on all disciplines, including the original Latin manuscript of Francis Bacon's *New Atlantis*, the utopian vision on which the American forefathers had allegedly modeled a new world based on ancient knowledge.

Perhaps the most famous work in the Folger Shakespeare collection is the first collected edition of Shakespeare's works, printed in 1623 and known as the First Folio. Out of a world supply of 238 First Folios, Folger collected seventy-nine copies, one of which is always on display in the Great Hall. He also acquired numerous copies of the Second, Third, and Fourth Folios, creating the world's largest collection of eighteenth- and nineteenth-century editions of Shakespeare, including copies owned by Washington, Adams, and Lincoln.

HOTEL OF PRESIDENTS

The Willard Hotel, first constructed in 1850 and extensively rebuilt since then, has a famous guest roster. Since Franklin Pierce, every U.S. president has either stayed in the hotel or attended some function there.

The entire collection housed at the library consists of approximately 280,000 books and manuscripts, and 27,000 paintings, drawings, prints, and engravings. The library's north wall features nine elaborate bas reliefs of famous scenes from Shakespeare, by sculptor John Gregory. The Reading Room is open to scholars and graduate students only.

Freedom Plaza

Freedom Plaza, located at the corner of Pennsylvania Avenue and Thirteenth Street, is a large plaza with a raised platform inlaid with stones that map many of the streets of Washington, D.C., as the city's primary designer Pierre L'Enfant first envisioned them. It also includes one of the largest bronze medallions ever cast of the Great Seal.

The plaza, designed by architect Robert Venturi and landscape architect George Patton, was constructed in 1980 and also features quotes from a coterie of famous people about Washington, D.C.

Initially named Western Plaza, it was renamed Freedom Plaza in honor of Martin Luther King Jr., who wrote parts of his "I Have a Dream" speech in the nearby Willard Hotel. In 1988, a time capsule containing a Bible, a robe, and other relics of King's was planted at the site, with plans to reopen it January 15, 2088.

The John A. Wilson Building, the seat of the District of Columbia government, faces the plaza, as does the historic National Theatre, which has been visited by every U.S. president since Andrew Jackson. It plays a role in Dan Brown's novel *The Lost Symbol* because its centrality to several metro lines allows the hero and heroine to escape their pursuers.

SKELETONS IN THE CLOSET

In the Smithsonian, there is a massive vaulted display room furnished with animal skeletons, scientific display cases, glass jars with biological samples, archaeological artifacts, and plaster casts of prehistoric reptiles. However, the space does not contain—so far as we know—any secret scientific labs.

Smithsonian Museum Support Center

Because many of our forefathers were Deists, men who believed in God in a universal and open-minded way, they came to America seeking religious freedom, not theology. They wanted to create a spiritual utopia that reflected and sustained freedom of thought, education, and scientific advancement. They were seeking enlightenment, not strictures or scriptures.

As such, they had many admirers. James Smithson, a wealthy British scientist, admired the fledging nation's devotion to knowledge, wisdom, and science and believed so strongly in America's destiny that he donated his entire fortune for the construction of "an establishment for the increase and diffusion of knowledge." That first Smithson building, now the Smithsonian Museum Support Center, is one of the buildings in the National Mall, which also houses other Smithsonian Museums.

Constructed in 1855, located at 4210 Silver Hill Road, just outside D.C., its red Seneca Creek sandstone columns dominate the landscape near the Capitol. Because it has Gothic and Romanesque influences, the Smithsonian resembles a medieval castle.

In *The Lost Symbol*, hero Robert Langdon says almost incredulously that the Smithsonian houses more pieces than the famous Hermitage Museum in St. Petersburg, Russia; the Vatican Museum; and the New York Metropolitan Museum combined. In the novel, the museum consists of five interconnected pods, one of which houses the experimental lab of Katherine Solomon, a noetic scientist.

The International Spy Museum

This fascinating museum—the first and only public institution dedicated to espionage—houses the largest collection of spy artifacts in America. Its mission: "To educate the public about espionage in an engaging manner and to provide a dynamic context that fosters understanding of its important role in, and impact on, current and historic events." To that end, its exhibits boast everything from a coded letter written by Revolutionary War spy Benedict Arnold to high-tech twenty-first-century espionage toys. Priding itself on providing an interactive experience, the museum also hosts scavenger hunts, spy city tours, and the trademarked Spy at Night experience in which participants can role play spies on a secret mission. The museum's gift store sells camera ties, James Bond credit card lock-picking kits, and "Deny Everything" t-shirts, among other intriguing items.

SPOKEN LIKE A SPY

"The International Spy Museum is more than history—more than information or entertainment—its mission is to reflect the significance of intelligence as a critical component of national security."
—Milton Maltz, Founder and Chairman of the International Spy Museum

Astrological Symbols in Washington, D.C.

Even though the names of the planets and zodiacal signs date back to pagan times, medieval Masons sanctified and Christianized the mythology of symbols, which is why they included symbols when constructing their temples and other buildings in America. Without a doubt, the mythology of astrological stars and planets played a role in the planning and history of our national capital city. The Freemasons' spiritual training taught them to seek new meaning in ancient symbols, which explains why the architects drew upon stellar lore to create a sacred geometry for the layout of Washington, D.C. A stellar design was meant to reveal and support its ascent as the center of the world.

GET A CLUE!

In *The Lost Symbol*, author Dan Brown explains that the ancient Greeks would inscribe their secret information on clay tablets, shatter the tablets, and store each piece in a separate location. The secrets could only be decoded when all the pieces were collected to form a symbolon, which he believes led to our use of the word *symbol*. Modern cryptologists use this method, which they call *segmented cipher*, or a code broken into pieces. «

In point of fact, Washington, D.C., is the only city in the world to have more than twenty public zodiacs on statuary and buildings.

ZODIACS ACROSS AMERICA

Boston has three public zodiacs. The most striking is the atrium zodiac in the floor of the Public Library in Copley Square. Another, the Egypto-Babylonian zodiac painted by John Singer Sargent, appears on the ceiling of the second floor of the Public Library. New York has one gorgeous zodiac encircling the statue of Prometheus by Paul Manship in Rockefeller Plaza. Also, Grand Central Station has a stunning celestial panorama on the ceiling.

GARFIELD STATUE

John Quincy Adams Ward, a famous sculptor in the late 1800s, sculptured the statue of President James Garfield that is located on Jefferson Drive near the Capitol. What appears to be an entire bronze horoscope, with the planets, has been cast on the northern side of the platform.

ALBERT EINSTEIN'S STATUE

A bronze statue of Albert Einstein sits outside the National Academy of Sciences. Einstein is depicted contemplating a star-spangled horoscope, for April 22, 1979, the centennial of his birth, on the marble floor beneath his feet. His right foot rests on two mega-stars: Boötes and Hercules.

Behind his statute, embedded in the metal doors of the National Academy of Sciences building, are twelve signs of the zodiac, along with their corresponding symbols.

FEDERAL RESERVE BOARD BUILDING

Interior designer Sidney Waugh created two light fixtures for the Marion Eccles building in Washington, which houses the Federal Reserve. The fixtures are encircled by a ring of Steuben glass, on which appear the signs of the zodiac.

STARS FROM EGYPT?

In the 1800s, when most of Washington was constructed, Sirius was the only star known to have been featured in Egyptian hieroglyphics. Greeks and Egyptians used the placement of Sirius in the sky to orient the location of their temples. The five-star symbol that came to represent Sirius may have been the antecedent of the five-pointed star used in the American flag.

The star Regulus, little ruler, also known as the guiding star of the Eternal City, played a role in our nation's capital. Regulus is one of three stars that link Washington, D.C., with the stellar realms.

House of the Temple of Scottish Rite

The Temple of the Scottish Rite is known to its brethren as Heredom. This name is derived from the Greek word *hieros-domos* or holy house. (Heredom is also a mythical mountain in Scotland, which supposedly was the site of the first Masonic chapter.) Located at 1733 16th Street (one mile from the White House), the Temple of the Scottish Rite is one of the most striking monuments in the nation's capital. The building, designed by John Russell Pope, who also designed the National Archives and the Jefferson Memorial, was constructed between 1911 and 1915 to headquarter the Supreme Council of the Southern Jurisdiction of the 33rd Degree of the Ancient and Accepted Rite of Freemasonry.

Pope modeled the temple after the tomb of King Mausolus at Halicarnassus, one of the seven wonders of the ancient world, and reportedly the building's nine-foot-thick walls hold human remains. The building is constructed entirely of stone, as the ancients would have done. In another nod to ancient Egypt, a pair of monumental seventeen-ton sphinxes, representing wisdom and power, guard the door. Inside, Egyptian hieroglyphics adorn a soaring atrium. The massive limestone facade is ringed with thirty-three Ionic columns. In the Temple Room, where Masons from around the world gather every two years, bronze coiling snakes flank a large wooden throne, canopied in purple velvet. Other symbols include nine-pointed stars, two-headed eagles, and images of the Greek god Hermes. In 1935, Franklin Delano Roosevelt, an esteemed Mason, donated funds for a stained-glass window featuring the ancient Egyptian "all-seeing eye."

O BEAUTIFUL FOR SCOTTISH RITE

In 1931, the temple was voted the fifth most beautiful building in the world by a group of members from the Association of American Architects. It became one of the most respected classical American designs of its time.

The dark green marble floors of the atrium lead to a grand staircase and a bronze bust of Masonic luminary Albert Pike, which bears this plaque: WHAT WE HAVE DONE FOR OURSELVES ALONE DIES WITH US; WHAT WE HAVE DONE FOR OTHERS AND THE WORLD REMAINS

AND IS IMMORTAL. Albert Pike was a former Confederate general who spent thirty-two years developing Masonic rituals, garnering his fair share of detractors (see Chapter 3). In 1944 the Masons, by an act of Congress, gained permission to dig up Pike's remains from a local cemetery and bury them in the temple.

Among the artifacts on display is a Masonic membership certificate signed by Paul Revere. The silversmith reportedly recruited some brethren for the Boston Tea Party in 1773. The banquet hall includes a large portrait of George Washington laying the cornerstone for the Capitol. He is wearing a Masonic apron. Scores of portraits of famous Masons—Sam Ervin, John Glenn, Harry Truman, Arnold Palmer, John Wayne, and Will Rogers among others—line a curving mahogany corridor. On the first floor is the reconstructed office of FBI director and Mason J. Edgar Hoover.

THE TEMPLE ROOM

The Temple Room is a perfect square with a 100-foot ceiling supported by eight monolithic, green granite, Doric-style columns. A tiered gallery of dark Russian walnut chairs with hand-tooled pigskin seats encircles the room. A thirty-three-foot-tall throne dominates the western wall, with a concealed pipe organ opposite it. (One of the few supposedly secret winding staircases leads up to the organ room.) The walls feature a kaleidoscope of ancient symbols: Egyptian, Hebraic, astronomical, alchemical, and some that remain mysterious.

In *The Lost Symbol*, Dan Brown describes the room as a hybrid sepulcher, with Greco-Roman-Egyptian influences such as black marble statues, chandelier fire bowls, Teutonic crosses, double-headed phoenix medallions, and sconces bearing the head of Hermes. Robert Langdon marvels at an enormous polished Belgian black marble altar located in the center of the room, under the oculus in the ceiling that radiates sunlight and moonlight onto the altar.

Brown also mentions a chair with two words carved across its back: KNOW THYSELF. Brown links this to the ancient wisdom that humans have forgotten that they are divine—that they are God. Robert Langdon postulates to Katherine Solomon that perhaps we will realize this when our science catches up with the wisdom of the ancients.

GET A CLUE!

A very common image in metaphorical symbolism, a portal represents a transformative rite of passage that one must go through to achieve enlightenment, to reach the Gate of Heaven. The idea of a mystical portal is a recurring mythological image that dates back to the Ancient Mysteries when allegory, myths, and symbols held powerful meanings.

In *The Lost Symbol,* a hexagonal coffer in the Capitol Dome actually swings open like a portal. The protagonist notes that it is a "figurative portal" representing a metaphorical gateway. «

THE LIBRARY

The Temple Library, the first public library in the District of Columbia, contains one of the world's largest collections of materials on and by Scottish poet Robert Burns, who was a Freemason. The library was opened to the public at the request of Albert Pike, who donated his personal collection of books with the stipulation that they be available for use, free of charge, by the general public.

Today it also houses more than 250,000 books, including a rare volume of *Ahiman Rezon, The Secrets of a Prepared Brother.* (This is a book of Masonic constitutions, written by

Laurence Dermott in the late eighteenth century. It holds a position of great importance in Masonic thought.) It also houses Masonic jewels, ritual artifacts, and even a rare volume that had been hand-printed by Benjamin Franklin. In *The Lost Symbol*, Robert Langdon views a library desk and a golden table lamp in the reading room that create the optical illusion of a pyramid with a gold capstone.

THE ARCHIVES

Unlike the library, the temple's private archives house the official records of the Scottish Rite and have long been solely a private resource for the Supreme Council. However, if you can prove that you are a bona fide Masonic scholar or researcher, you can access the archive—if the Grand Archivist approves your request to do so.

Some 2 million items are stored in archival cases and fireproof file drawers. The second main storage area is the Archives Vault, which contains the most valuable documents, manuscripts, and books, published and unpublished. Unfortunately, soon after the founding of the Supreme Council, some of the earliest documents were lost in a fire or through the death of leaders. When Albert Pike joined the Supreme Council, he was horrified to learn that many valuable documents had been given to other jurisdictions and never returned or were buried in a jumble of disorganization. Pike worked toward creating an archivist system, by systematically examining and cataloguing every document in the Archives, a chore that continues to this day.

George Washington Masonic Memorial

In Alexandria, Virginia, atop Shuter's Hill, the George Washington Masonic Memorial, which is one of the most famous

Masonic structures in America, features three distinct tiers of increasingly complex architecture. It features Doric influences on the bottom tier, Ionic on the second tier, and Corinthian on the third tier. Inspired by the ancient lighthouse of Alexandria, Egypt, it was designed to represent man's intellectual ascent. Like that lighthouse it is topped by a pyramid with a filial designed to resemble a flame.

Inside is a massive bronze statue of George Washington in full Masonic regalia, along with the trowel he used to lay the cornerstone of the Capitol Building. Above the foyer, nine levels bear names like the Grotto, the Crypt Room, and the Knights Templar Chapel. The building houses more than 20,000 volumes of Masonic writings, a replica of the Ark of the Covenant, and a scale model of the throne room in King Solomon's Temple.

WASHINGTON'S MASONIC CAREER

George Washington was most associated with two lodges: Fredericksburg Lodge at Fredericksburg, Virginia, which was his Mother Lodge, and Alexandria-Washington Lodge at Alexandria, Virginia. Washington was initiated an Entered Apprentice on November 4, 1752, at the Fredericksburg Lodge, passed to Fellowcraft on March 3, 1753, and was raised to Master Mason on August 4, 1753.

Washington attended a St. John the Baptist Celebration at the Alexandria Lodge in June 1784. He was later made an Honorary Member of the Lodge. On April 22, 1788, and when the Lodge received a Charter from the Grand Lodge of Virginia as Alexandria Lodge No. 22, they asked Washington to serve as Charter Master under the Virginia Charter and he agreed. Washington was inaugurated as the First President of the United States on April 30, 1789, while holding the office of Master of Alexandria Lodge. After his death on December 14,

1799, the Lodge was renamed Alexandria-Washington Lodge No. 22 by the Grand Lodge of Virginia.

Through the generosity of Washington's family and friends, Alexandria-Washington Lodge became the repository of many artifacts of Washington and the Washington family. The Lodge rooms were inadequate for the display and storage of the memorabilia, and fire in the Lodge in 1871 destroyed many of the invaluable and significant Washington artifacts.

In 1909, after receiving the gift of land on Shuter's Hill for a fireproof lodge, Joseph W. Eggleston, the Grand Master of Virginia, invited every Grand Master in the United States to assemble in Alexandria-Washington Lodge on February 22, 1910, to plan the George Washington Masonic National Memorial Association.

A FITTING MEMORIAL

Ten years later, the Grand Lodges of the United States finally approved the concept of a colossal building as a memorial "lighthouse" to Washington. The site followed the ancient tradition for the location of temples on hilltops or mountains. It was also located on the very spot once proposed by Thomas Jefferson as the ideal site for the nation's Capitol.

On November 1, 1923, the memorial's cornerstone was dedicated in a Masonic ceremony. President Calvin Coolidge, former President and Chief Justice William H. Taft, and numerous other dignitaries performed the ceremony before a crowd of thousands of Freemasons from around the nation. For more than ten years, even through the Depression when most construction ground to a halt, Freemasons steadily and faithfully contributed to the construction of the memorial. On May 12, 1932, the bicentennial year of George Washington's birth, the dedication of the Memorial took place with President Herbert Hoover participating.

After World War II, work on the Memorial's interior began in earnest. By 1970, the George Washington Masonic Memorial was completed. In 1999, the large square and compasses were added to the front lawn, a visible sign to the Masonic nature of the memorial. A repository of many artifacts and the history of American Freemasons, the memorial remains a lasting monument to George Washington, Father of our Country and Mason.

Potomac Lodge No. 5

On April 21, 1789, at a meeting in Easton, Talbot County, Maryland, as George Washington was making his way to New York City to be inaugurated, the Grand Lodge of Maryland granted the petition of "a number of respectable brethren from George Town on the Patowmack River," and issued a charter establishing Lodge No. 9 of Maryland. Today it is known as Potomac Lodge No. 5, located in Georgetown, and it is the oldest Masonic lodge in D.C., Mother Lodge for the Masonic forefathers who laid the cornerstone for the White House and the Capitol Building.

THE FALLEN HERO OF POTOMAC LODGE NO. 5

Leslie Coffelt of Potomac Lodge No. 5 was killed in the line of duty as a Washington, D.C., police officer in January 1950. He died protecting President Harry S. Truman, a 33rd Degree Mason, from two Puerto Rican terrorists who opened fire on the President in front of the Blair House, where he and his wife were living while the White House was being repaired. The Mason Bartender

Unfortunately, the Lodge minutes from April 21, 1789, to 1795 were destroyed in a fire, but it has been well authenticated that President Washington, President Thomas Jefferson, the Marquis de LaFayette, and Major Pierre L'Enfant all visited this Lodge, which met at Suter's Fountain Inn for several years after it was chartered.

The historic George Washington Gavel was among the Masonic implements used by Worshipful Brother Washington when he performed the ceremonial cornerstone laying for the United States Capitol building on September 18, 1793, as Worshipful Master of Alexandria-Washington Lodge No. 22 of Virginia. Also participating in the ceremony were Lodge No. 9 of Maryland (now Potomac Lodge No. 5) and Lodge No. 15 of Maryland (now Federal Lodge No. 1, FAAM, of D.C.).

At the conclusion of the ceremony, President Washington gave the silver trowel he used to his own Lodge, Alexandria-Washington No. 22 of Virginia, and presented the gavel to the Worshipful Master of Lodge No. 9 of Maryland, Valentine Reintzel. It is likely that the gavel was given to Lodge No. 9 because it was the older of the two Maryland Lodges participating in the ceremony.

WASHINGTON'S MASONIC GAVEL

The head of the Washington Gavel is made of the same Maryland marble originally used in the interior of the Capitol, and its handle is crafted of a dark American cherry of unique grain. John Duffy, a silversmith and a Freemason, specially crafted the gavel and the other Masonic tools used during the ceremonies for the Capitol Building. Duffy was married to a daughter of President Washington's gardener.

Reintzel, who in 1811 became the first Grand Master of the Grand Lodge of Free and Accepted Masons of the District of Columbia, retained personal possession of the gavel until his death in 1817. At that time his family returned the gavel to the Lodge, where it was kept under lock and key until 1922, when it was moved to Riggs National Bank (now PNC Bank), where it rests today in a specially constructed box of their deposit vault. Luckily, the gavel was safely in the bank when the Lodge Hall, then across the street from the bank at 1210 Wisconsin Avenue, N.W., burned to the ground in 1963, destroying most of the Lodge's records and artifacts.

WASHINGTON'S VAULT BOX

The vault box that holds Washington's gavel was constructed with a glass door and centrally located in the vault so that visitors to the bank would be able to view the gavel when the vault was open. The construction of such a safe deposit box was unique at its time, and the Lodge remains unaware of any other glass-faced security deposit box in any other bank.

The Secret Code of Equestrian Statues

Washington, D.C., is laden with equestrian statues—from the Ulysses S. Grant Memorial west of the Capitol building to the Joan of Arc statue at Meridian Hill Park. Is there a secret code that exists among the designers of equestrian statues? Depending on the position of the hooves, believers say you can tell how the rider died.

- All four hooves on the ground means a peaceful death.
- One hoof off the ground means the rider was injured in battle (but did not necessarily die from his injuries).

- Two hooves off the ground means the rider died in battle.

A review of equestrian statues in Washington, D.C., shows that only about one-third of the statues follow this "rule," so it appears to be more of a case of trying to find a pattern where none exits. Case in point: Major General Andrew Jackson died peacefully, despite the fact that his horse is depicted rearing.

Another rumored statue code is said to exist on Monument Avenue in Richmond, Virginia, where the statues of civil war heroes are said to face North if they died in the war and South if they survived. Alas, this too applies only to a small number of the statues. Nice theory, but not accurate.

MORE MASONIC SITES IN WASHINGTON, D.C.

As we've seen, our nation's capital city is rich in Masonic art and architecture—both overt and convert. Here's a list of other notable places of interest:

- Almas Shrine Temple, home of The Ancient Arabic Order of Nobles of the Mystic Shrine on Franklin Square
- Freemasonry Museum at the Grand Lodge of District of Columbia
- Prince Hall Grand Lodge of District of Columbia
- Collingwood Library and Museum, repository of 4,500 books on history and Freemasonry
- Museum of Women in the Arts, originally built as a Masonic temple in 1908
- Naval Lodge #4, the oldest Masonic edifice in D.C.

Conclusion: We're Not in Kansas Anymore

As we've seen in this chapter, Washington, D.C., is overflowing with places rich in the secret symbolism of the Ancient Mysteries, Freemasonry, and more. But it's not the only place in our great nation where you can find such influences. In the next chapter, we'll take an intriguing road tour of our country—one surreptitious landmark at a time.

CHAPTER 11
THE SECRET PLACES OF AMERICA

Ebert County, Georgia. Sandusky, Ohio. Philadelphia, Pennsylvania. Lake Havasu City, Arizona. No matter where you are in this great nation, you can find traces of the Ancient Mysteries. From the thirteen original colonies to the wide expanses of the Wild West, there are places steeped in the search for the divine truth and light. Let's take a tour of these often unlikely and unexpected repositories of secrets.

The Chancellor Robert R. Livingston Masonic Library, New York City

This library, located at 71 West Twenty-Third Street, is one of the world's foremost repositories of Masonic books, artifacts, and ephemera available to visitors and researchers. Among its artifacts is a rare and highly significant transcript of the *Processus Contra Templarios*, a publication containing a collection of facsimile manuscripts relating to the trials of the Knights Templar in the Middle Ages. Historians used a "Wood's lamp" or ultraviolet light to scrutinize the original documents, recovering sections that had never been seen.

THE "LOST" CHINON PARCHMENT

Using the lamp, investigators found the important document known as the Chinon Parchment, which contained Pope Clement V's absolution of the Templars, thwarting King Philip of France's crusade to eliminate them. Historians had been searching for the Chinon Parchmont for centuries to no avail. When the Vatican made the documents available in 2001, it said the Chinon Parchment apparently had been "incorrectly catalogued" by the Vatican in centuries long past.

The Livingston Masonic Library obtained the manuscripts when, concurrent with the seven hundredth anniversary of the Knights Templar, the Vatican Secret Archives finally published 800 copies of the previously unavailable source material on the hearings that eventually exonerated the Knights Templar of heresy.

The Livingston Masonic Library may be the only Masonic-affiliated research facility to purchase a copy, and it now owns one of the few available in the United States. Although the Masons deny a true historical link between the medieval Knights Templar and modern Freemasonry (and no one has ever proved that such a link exists), they do recognize the Knights Templar as "an inspiration." Therefore, they purchased the documents to provide material for researchers tracing the history of the Freemasons, both factual and imaginative.

Federal Hall, 26 Wall Street, New York City

This site, where our first president took his oath of office, currently houses the Bible upon which George Washington swore to protect and defend the Constitution of the United States. At the time, this was the site of New York City's eighteenth-century City Hall. During the years that New York was the national capital, Pierre L'Enfant had been hired to remodel the City Hall building for the new federal government, but when the capital moved to Philadelphia, the building was once again used to house the city government until it was demolished in 1812. The current building served as a Customs House from 1842 to 1862, when it became the U.S. Sub-Treasury. Millions of dollars of gold and silver were secreted in basement vaults until 1920, when the Federal Reserve Bank replaced the Sub-Treasury.

When George Washington stood on a platform in front of the building to take the Oath of Office on April 30, 1789, and the officials noticed that they had not procured a Bible, they began a frantic search for a Holy Bible. Jacob Morton, a member of St. John's Lodge (which met at the Old Coffee House on the corner of Water and Wall Streets), dashed to the lodge to borrow their altar's Holy Bible.

THE BIBLE OF THE PRESIDENTS

This Holy Bible was a replica of the original Lodge Bible, which had been destroyed in a fire on March 8, 1770, along with the lodge's earliest records and furnishings. The Bible is the King James Version, complete with the Apocrypha and elaborately supplemented with the historical, astronomical, and legal data of that period. It contains numerous artistic steel engravings by the celebrated English artist John Stuart. These portray biblical narratives from designs and paintings by old masters.

The Bible has since been used at four other inaugurations:

- President Harding in 1921
- President Eisenhower in 1953
- President Jimmy Carter in 1977
- President George H. W. Bush in 1989

The Bible was also to have been used for the inauguration of George W. Bush in 2001, but rain prevented its use.

It has also been present at numerous public and Masonic occasions, including:

- Washington's funeral procession in New York City, December 31, 1799
- The introduction of Croton water into New York City, October 14, 1840
- The dedication of the Masonic Temple in Boston, June 24, 1867, and of that in Philadelphia on May 24, 1869
- The dedication of the Washington monument in Washington, D.C., February 21, 1885 and its rededication in 1998
- The laying of the cornerstone of the Masonic Home at Utica, New York, on May 21, 1891

St. Johns Lodge, Boston

Maybe it's not so mysterious, but it is a vital link in the Masonic chain and well worth a visit. It all began in 1733, when Anthony Lord Viscount Montague, Grand Master of the Grand Lodge of England, appointed Henry Price, a prominent Boston tailor and storekeeper, "Provincial Grand Master of New England and Dominions and Territories thereunto belonging." On July 30, 1733, at a meeting held at the Bunch of Grapes Tavern in Boston, Henry Price exercised his authority and granted a group of eighteen Masons a charter, making St. John's Lodge, the first duly constituted and chartered lodge in America.

St. John's Lodge has been in continuous existence ever since, convening for more than 3,700 regular meetings. Famous

Masons such as George Washington, Ben Franklin, and the Marquis de Lafayette visited St. John's Lodge in their travels to Boston. Other St. John's Masons include:

Josiah Quincy and **John Rowe,** whose names are affixed to the historical Quincy Market and Rowe's Wharf in Boston. It was Rowe who famously commented just before the Boston Tea Party, "One wonders how tea will mix with salt water."

James Otis, who argued against the Writs of Assistance in the 1760s, went on to coin the slogan "Taxation without representation is tyranny!" and is today credited as the Father of the Fourth Amendment.

Robert Newman, who climbed the Old North Church to signal "One if by land and two if by sea" on the orders of fellow Mason Paul Revere.

Lowell Thomas, the most prominent newsman of the 1920s and the reporter perhaps best remembered as the man who discovered and made Lawrence of Arabia famous.

FROM KING'S CHAPEL TO ANCIENT GREECE

An unauthorized Masonic lodge may have met in King's Chapel, Boston, as early as the 1720s, reportedly meeting according to the "old customs."

Reportedly, the Masons are currently rebuilding and refurbishing a pyramidal building in Washington, D.C., based on a Greek Mausoleum, adding new galleries for videos and displays of magnificent regalia to provide a coherent history of the origins, development, and meaning of Freemasonry.

National Heritage Museum, Lexington, Massachusetts

The Massachusetts Masons have loaned the National Heritage Museum close to 12,000 artifacts, including a gold urn and silver ladle crafted by Paul Revere, who was a Most Worshipful Master in the 1790s. The museum includes an exhibit featuring the highlights of the collection, followed by another exhibition that features anti-Masonic screeds from the last three centuries accusing members of plotting against royalty or propping up Communism.

The museum also houses a print of *Franklin Opening the Lodge*, dating back to 1896. The print depicts Franklin wearing a Masonic apron and a Master's jewel around his neck, while standing in a lodge room filled with Masonic symbols.

THE FIRST MASONIC BOOK PRINTED IN AMERICA

Another museum treasure associated with Benjamin Franklin is a rare copy of James Anderson's *The Constitutions of the Free-Masons*, the first Masonic book printed in America. Through typographical forensics, such as noting a series of ads published in Benjamin Franklin's *Pennsylvania Gazette* advertising the book "Reprinted by B. Franklin," Masonic historians believe Benjamin Franklin printed the book in 1734, while he was Grand Master of Pennsylvania. The book was reprinted from the first edition published in 1723 in London. Nowhere in the book did Franklin credit himself with being its printer. A facsimile of this edition is available online through the University of Nebraska-Lincoln, *http://digitalcommons.unl.edu/libraryscience/25/.*

Philadelphia, Pennsylvania

Since Benjamin Franklin was one of the premier Masons in colonial America, you'd expect there to be some important

Masonic sites associated with his home town of Philadelphia. And you'd be right.

IN THE BEGINNING . . .

The Right Worshipful Grand Lodge of the most Ancient and Honorable Fraternity of Free and Accepted Masons is one of the oldest such lodges in the United States. It was established just ten years after the start of the Revolution, in 1786. However, another lodge in the city was created even earlier. The earliest lodge known to have been established in North America was at the Tun Tavern in Philadelphia. The tavern was a brew house, built in 1685, and the Masonic lodge dates to at least 1731 and may be even older.

A TUN OF FUN

A *tun* is a cask built to hold beer or wine, usually containing a bit more than 250 gallons. For this reason, alehouses in Britain and its colonies were often named Tun—sometimes Three Tun or Two Tun, depending on the amount of spirits the proprietor had on hand.

The tavern was the site of other historic events, including the founding of the United States Marine Corps in 1775. The founder of the corps was, incidentally, the grandson of a Mason.

Today, the Pennsylvania Grand Lodge Temple is the center of Freemason life in the City of Brotherly Love.

THE FRANKLIN INSTITUTE

Featured in the movie *National Treasure,* the Franklin Institute is dedicated to displaying the all-encompassing genius of Benjamin Franklin. It includes a science museum and research institute, as well as the Franklin Memorial.

IT'S ELECTRIFYING!

In 1893, the eccentric genius and inventor Nikola Tesla first demonstrated wireless telegraphy at the Franklin Institute. Tesla (1856–1943) worked extensively in both Paris and Philadelphia, two cities greatly influenced by Franklin.

Sandusky, Ohio

Sandusky's claim to fame is that it and Washington, D.C., are the *only two cities* in the country whose infrastructure was laid out on Masonic symbols. Why Sandusky? The apparent reason is that Hector Kilbourne, a surveyor and the first Worshipful Master of the Sandusky Masonic Lodge, designed the city of Sandusky's streets by creating a grid pattern, known as the Kilbourne Plat, overlaying streets to resemble the symbols of Freemasonry. He recorded the map on the Fourth of July in 1818. The streets form the compass and square. Main city streets such as Central, Huron, Poplar, and Elm cut in at an angle toward Sandusky Bay and Lake Erie, creating sharply angled intersections. The two main arms of the compass, Central and Huron, don't actually meet at a point but now feature a flowered, inner-city park, maintained by the Masonic Lodge and featuring gardens in the shape of the compass and square. The Masonic Science Lodge on Columbus Avenue sits in the middle of the compass, where it overlooks a monument to Kilbourne.

Up to the turn of the twentieth century, the Masons were a huge force in the city. City officials were Masons and reportedly parceled out jobs to fellow members. As immigrants flooded the country, the influence of the Masonic lodges diminished, though the Science Lodge still has approximately 500 members. As to why so many Masons ended up in Sandusky, perhaps it can be traced to the influx of Connecticut citizens who were burned out by the British in the Revolutionary War. In 1792, 500,000 acres of land, now known as the Firelands, were set aside in Sandusky for the displaced refugees.

WHAT ELSE YOU DIDN'T KNOW ABOUT SANDUSKY

Prior to the abolition of slavery, Sandusky was a major stop on the Underground Railroad, where slaves would board boats crossing Lake Erie to Ontario.

For those interested in Native American languages and cultures, and the early interactions between those peoples and the European settlers, the Sandusky Library Archives Research Center houses a manuscript, dated 1787, of a phrase book containing translations of words, phrases, and speeches from English to a local Native American language, possibly the Wyandot/Huron language. The manuscript is attributed to E. R. Jewett, but the accuracy of this claim is cloudy since the only signatures with the Jewett name are written in pencil along the margin of a page and don't seem to match the rest of the handwriting. Although access to the original item is restricted due to its age and fragility, the entire document (twenty-one leaves on thirty-two digital images) is available in digital format at the library.

Harvey Keitel plays an F.B.I. agent named Agent Sandusky in the movie *National Treasure*.

The Jackson House, Newton, Massachusetts

William Jackson's house in Newton, Massachusetts, was a "station" on the Underground Railroad. The Jacksons were abolitionists, people who worked to end slavery. Today, the Jackson House is a museum with a large collection of historical objects and documents that are used for research into Newton's past.

UNDERGROUND RAILROAD

If you were an escaped slave before the Civil War, the best way to travel was along the Underground Railroad. This wasn't a real railroad but a secret system of "safe houses" located throughout the Northern states. The system helped escaped slaves from the South reach places of safety in the North or in Canada, often called the "Promised Land" because U.S. slave laws could not be enforced there. The slaves frequently wore disguises and traveled in darkness on the "railroad." Railway terms were used in the secret system: Routes were called *lines*, stopping places were called *stations*, and people who helped escaped slaves along the way were *conductors*. One of the most famous conductors on the Underground Railroad was Harriet Tubman, a former slave who escaped from Maryland.

Stone Mountain, Georgia

Stone Mountain, often (inaccurately) billed as the "largest exposed piece of granite in the world," is actually a 683-foot-high piece of quartz monzonite that at one time was called the Crystal Mountain, because many believed it was studded with precious gems. The United States purchased it from the Creek Indians in the 1820s, and later, through private ownership, the site became a used granite quarry and tourist attraction.

In May 1914, an Atlanta attorney named William H. Terrell suggested in an *Atlanta Constitution* editorial that Stone Mountain should be used as a memorial to the Confederacy. Within days Caroline Helen Jemison Plane, founder of the Georgia Division and Atlanta Chapter of the United Daughters of the Confederacy, took up the sword, proposing that they sculpt a monument of Robert E. Lee. At that time, Sam Venable owned the property, and he suggested that the committee commission sculptor John de la Mothe Gutzon Borglum to carve a monument on the mountain.

From 1916 to 1923, economic constrictions almost ground construction to a halt until a group of Atlanta business and civic leaders formed an association to accumulate funds to pay their debts and complete the memorial sculpture.

By this time both Venable and Borglum's association with the Ku Klux Klan was well known, as were their attempts to stack the Association's board with Klan members. Eventually Borglum had a falling-out with the original sponsors, who were not happy that he had also accepted a commission to sculpt Mount Rushmore. In February 1925, the committee canceled Borglum's contract. In a fury, Borglum drove to his studio, destroyed his models, and fled the state. The Association filed charges for "malicious mischief," but when they located the sculptor in North Carolina, they discovered that they couldn't extradite him on a misdemeanor, so they also created a felony charge of larceny. North Carolinians refused extradition, and the charges against Borglum were eventually dropped.

Later that same year, the Association hired Augustus Lukeman, a Virginia sculptor who discarded Borglum's design and proposed a new design. He envisioned two groups, one of four men on horseback, Robert E. Lee, Jefferson Davis, "Stonewall" Jackson, and an unnamed color-bearer. The second group would later be dropped, and the Lee, Davis, Jackson group would form the monument. Lukeman's head of General Lee was unveiled in April 1928. However, shortly after this unveiling, the work ceased due to the Association's lack of money.

THE CARVING COMPLETED

In 1958, the Georgia Legislature set up the Stone Mountain Memorial Association (SMMA) and gave it authority to purchase the mountain and surrounding areas for a state park. Because Venable had deeded rights to the Klan to hold meetings on the mountain, the state took the drastic measure of condemning their own land as a way to relieve the state of this unfortunate stigma In 1963, Walker Kirtland Hancock was hired to complete Lukeman's design, and on May 9, 1970, the completed carving was finally unveiled.

Ironically, when the dedication occurred in May 1970, William Holmes Borders, a noted African-American theologian and pastor of the Wheat Ave. Baptist Church, was tapped to give the invocation, a move that forced the Klan to give up plans of attending the ceremony.

THE GENERAL'S ELBOW

The recess just behind General Lee's left elbow is nearly twelve inches deep into the mountain. The butt of his horse is large enough to park a full-sized school bus on.

Mount Rushmore, South Dakota

Originally, the location of Mount Rushmore in the Black Hills was sacred land, known as Six Grandfathers to the Lakota Sioux. The U.S. government seized control of the mountain after several military conflicts, after which it was known by several different names, including Slaughterhouse Mountain.

In 1924, South Dakota state historian Doane Robinson came up with the idea of carving a massive sculpture into the Black Hills as a way to lure tourists to the struggling state. He invited Gutzon Borglum to sculpt Western heroes such as Lewis and Clark, Chief Red Cloud, and Buffalo Bill into the face of the hills.

As noted earlier, Borglum had come under fire for his affiliation with the Ku Klux Kan and fled the Stone Mountain project. He accepted the commission for the Black Hills but rejected Robinson's idea, replacing it with what he termed "a shrine to democracy." (Others, less charitable, say Borglum envisioned it as a monument to the white men who had tamed the West.)

Borglum's vision included carving the presidents, as well as a "secret" 80-foot-by-100-foot Hall of Records: a vault to house the Declaration of Independence and the U.S. Constitution, as well as a record of American history, including insight into how and why the memorial was built.

Borglum's full vision went unfulfilled until 1998, when the park service placed a teak box housed in a titanium vault in a hole they drilled at the hall's entrance. Located beyond a high-security fence, a set of steep metal steps leads to an oblong sliver, resembling the secret entrance to a pharaoh's tomb. The vault contains sixteen porcelain enamel panels that feature the text of the Declaration of Independence and the Constitution, biographies of the four presidents on the monument, as well as of Borglum, and the history of the United States. The capsule is sealed with a granite capstone.

MOUNT RUSHMORE'S SACRED PAST

Paha Sapa, meaning *Black Hills* in Lakota, was—and remains—a sacred landscape to many Native American nations, some of whom regard them as the center of the world. Natural formations such as Bear Butte and the Devil's Tower (over the border in Wyoming) are the setting for prayers, vision quests, and healing ceremonies, while Wind Cave, a vast underground complex of limestone tunnels, is revered as the place where the Lakota emerged from the underworld to Earth.

Under the 1868 Treaty of Fort Laramie, Congress agreed that the area would remain inviolate as the core of the Greater Sioux Reservation. But only six years later, President Ulysses S. Grant ordered a military "reconnaissance" into the region, possibly due to rumors of gold in the mountains. Lt. Col. George Armstrong Custer led a small army of more than 1,000 men, including cavalry and infantry, Indian scouts, interpreters, guides, and civilian scientists, into the region with more than 100 canvas wagons, three Gatling guns, and a cannon. Unfortunately, Custer's prospectors discovered gold in the mountains, and soon a rush to the Black Hills was on, with Deadwood, in the northern part of the region, one of the first illegal settlements.

President Grant sent envoys to buy the Black Hills, but the Lakota refused to bargain: Lakota Chief Sitting Bull said he would not sell so much as a pinch of dust. In the Great Sioux War that broke out in 1876 between the United States and a combined force of Lakota, Northern Cheyenne, and Arapaho tribes, many of the cavalrymen lost their lives at the Little Bighorn River in Montana—including Custer and Calhoun. The Lakota, however, were soon defeated, and in 1877 Congress passed an act requiring them to relinquish their land and stay on reservations.

SACRED AT ANY PRICE

In 1980 a court ruling awarded the Sioux more than $100 million for the loss of the Hills, but to date the Lakota have refused the money, which has grown with interest to well over $500 million.

CRAZY HORSE'S SWEET REVENGE

In the late 1930s, Lakota Chief Henry Standing Bear invited a Boston sculptor, Korczak Ziolkowski, to undertake a massive sculpture of Crazy Horse to be located only fifteen miles from Mount Rushmore. World War II intervened, so construction didn't begin until 1948, when Ziolkowski leased a vast chunk of the Black Hills and began sculpting a 563-foot-tall sculpture of the famous Native American. When finished, the sculpture will be the world's largest mountain carving—dwarfing such monuments as the Great Pyramid of Giza and the Statue of Liberty—capable of housing all four of Rushmore's presidents, each of which is as high as a six-story building, inside Crazy Horse's 87.5-foot-tall head. To prevent the U.S. government from becoming involved in the project, Ziolkowski funded the project with private donations and contributions from visitors. When Ziolkowski died in 1982, his family rallied to continue the work. Although the carving is still in process, more than 1 million tourists already flock to the site every year.

THE THOEN STONE

Visitors to the Adams Museum in Deadwood, South Dakota, are invited to view the Thoen Stone, an artifact whose discovery (or creation) dates to 1887. Louis Thoen, a Mason, said he discovered the stone in a cave near Spearfish and claimed someone named Ezra Kind had etched a message on the stone—while being pursued by hostile Indians—confirming that a party of seven prospectors found gold in the Hills, but all but Kind had been killed. Despite serious doubts about the stone's authenticity, there is ample evidence that explorers and mountain men did know about the presence of gold in the Black Hills as early as the 1820s, long before General Armstrong Custer's expedition to the Black Hills in 1874.

In yet another ironic twist, in 2004 Gerard Baker, a Mandan-Hidatsa raised on the Fort Berthold Reservation in western North Dakota, became Mount Rushmore's first American Indian superintendent. Baker, fifty-two, has begun to expand programs and lectures at the monument to include the Indian perspective. Until recently, visitors learned about Rushmore as a patriotic symbol, as a work of art, or as a geological formation, but nothing about its pre-white history—or why it raises such bitterness among many Native Americans. In fact, a lot of Indian people look at Mount Rushmore as a symbol of what white people did to this country when they arrived—took the land from the Indians and desecrated it.

Georgia's Stonehenge

In June 1979, an elegant gray-haired man calling himself Robert C. Christian met first with Joe Hendley, president of Elberton Granite Finishing Company, located in Elberton, Georgia, the "granite capital of the world." Mr. Christian revealed that he wished to construct a massive granite structure that would serve as a calendar, a clock, and a compass. He noted that it had to be strong enough to endure catastrophic events, so anyone who survived would be able to use the guides he wanted carved into the stone to create a better civilization than the one that Mr. Christian noted was "on the brink of self-destruction."

At first, Hendley thought the man was loony, but he began to take him seriously as Christian described the scope of the project in detail. When Christian asked for a referral to a trustworthy banker, Hendley sent him to Wyatt Martin, president of the Granite City Bank, to arrange financing. Once there, the well-dressed, soft-spoken stranger informed Martin that he and a small group of "loyal Americans who believe in God and country" had been planning for twenty years to "secretly" finance and construct a massive monument to the conservation of humanity. He told Martin that Robert C. Christian was a pseudonym and asked Martin to sign a confidentiality agreement that would bind him to never reveal Mr. Christian's true identity and to destroy all the documents and records related to the project upon its completion. Like Hendley, Martin was impressed with Mr. Christian but remained skeptical. On his second visit, however, Mr. Christian gave Hendley a shoebox containing a wooden model of the monument and ten or more pages of detailed specifications. A few days later he sent a $10,000 deposit to Martin.

THE MONUMENT

The Georgia Guidestones, also sometimes called the American Stonehenge for their similarity to the inner circle of Stonehenge, consists of four granite slabs in a paddle-wheel design. In the middle, a stone pillar holds a square capstone, which also touches the four panels. A 100-foot crane was used to lift the stones into place. The monument's total weight is approximately 240,000 pounds, and it was constructed so it can track the sun's east-west migration throughout the year, thusly:

> A carefully cut slot in the center column will frame the sunrise during equinoxes or solstices.

> An eye-level opening offers a clear view of Polaris, better known as the North Star.

> A ⅞-inch opening drilled through the capstone allows sunbeams to pinpoint the day of the year at noon.

A narrowly focused rocket motor was used to cut and finish huge blue granite slabs acquired from Pyramid Quarry. Master stonecutters smoothed the stones. The stones were then trucked to the site, a flat-topped hill with vistas in all directions on the local Double 7 Farms' pasture, the highest point in rural Elberton, Georgia. Mr. Christian selected the site to keep costs low, to take advantage of the mild Georgia weather, and because Elberton was considered by local Native Americans as the center of the world.

THE GUIDESTONES' PHYSICAL STATISTICS

Outer stones	42,437 pounds each
Center stone	20,957 pounds
Capstone	24,832 pounds
Overall Height:	19 feet 3 inches (Stonehenge is 13 feet)

Ten dictates or guides are carved into both faces of the outer stones, in eight languages:

- English
- Spanish
- Swahili
- Hindi
- Hebrew
- Arabic
- Chinese
- Russian

"Let these be guidestones to an age of reason" is carved on the sides of the capstone in four archaic languages:

- Babylonian Cuneiform
- Classical Greek
- Egyptian Hieroglyphics
- Sanskrit

THE TEN GUIDES

The "commandments" on the stone are as follows:

1. Maintain humanity under 500,000,000 in perpetual balance with nature.
2. Guide reproduction wisely—improving fitness and diversity.
3. Unite humanity with a living new language.
4. Rule passion—faith—tradition—and all things with tempered reason.
5. Protect people and nations with fair laws and just courts.
6. Let all nations rule internally resolving external disputes in a world court.
7. Avoid petty laws and useless officials.
8. Balance personal rights with social duties.
9. Prize truth—beauty—love—seeking harmony with the infinite.
10. Be not a cancer on the earth—leave room for nature— leave room for nature.

Upon completion of construction, Mr. Christian bade a permanent farewell to Hendley. For years, he communicated with Martin from various cities across the globe, even after transferring ownership of the land and the monument to Elbert County.

WHO WAS MR. CHRISTIAN?

The mysterious stranger and the monument's similarity to Stonehenge led to much speculation in the community. Some people accused Hendley and Martin of concocting the story and creating the monument as a self-aggrandizing publicity stunt. The venom grew so vicious that Hendley and Martin both voluntarily took and passed lie detector tests. Still, some accused them of doing the devil's work. A local minister warned that occult groups would conduct sacrifices on the Georgia Guidestones. To add to the mystery, Charlie Clamp, the man who sandblasted the 4,000 characters on the stones, said he had often heard "strange music and disjointed voices" when performing his craft.

ENTER THE WITCHES

Soon after the monument was unveiled, on the vernal equinox on March 22, 1980, a coven of Atlanta-based witches began weekend pilgrimages to Elberton to conduct pagan rites, mostly involving dancing and chanting. Reportedly, at least one warlock-witch marriage ceremony occurred. No human sacrifices have taken place, but some say chickens have been sacrificed, or at least separated from their heads.

The media searched for the elusive Mr. Christian but consistently came up empty-handed. Interest eventually died down but was revived briefly when Yoko Ono contributed a track called "Georgia Stone" to a tribute album for avant-garde composer John Cage. One verse of the song quotes the tenth and final guide: "Be not a cancer on Earth—leave room for nature—leave room for nature."

The only person to ever see Mr. Christian was the banker Martin, who would meet Mr. Christian for dinner when he passed through Atlanta. When pressed for information, Mr. Christian would quote Henry James's observation of Stonehenge: "You may put a hundred questions to these rough-hewn giants as they bend in grim contemplation of their fallen companions, but your curiosity falls dead in the vast sunny stillness that enshrouds them." Martin reportedly received his last communiqué from Mr. Christian right around the time of the 9/11 terrorist attack, but he assumes the now elderly Mr. Christian has most likely died.

GET A CLUE!

Although it remains a mystery, many conjecture that the famous stone circle known as Stonehenge on Salisbury Plain in England symbolized the cosmic eye of the Great Goddess or universal mother. Some stone circles were also used to map astronomical movements. «

THE NEW WORLD ORDER—OR SATANISTS?

In 1981, in an issue of the magazine *UFO Report*, a noted Atlanta psychic predicted that the true purpose of the Georgia Guidestones would be revealed in thirty years. She also noted that the Georgia Guidestones form an "X" that would make a perfect landing site for a UFO.

Mark Dice, author of *The Resistance Manifesto* (who also calls himself John Conner, in reference to the *Terminator* movies), demanded that the Georgia Guidestones be smashed into a million pieces. He conjectures that Mr. Christian was a high-ranking member of a "Luciferian secret society" at the forefront of a New World Order. He believes that the Georgia Guidestones are the New World Order's Ten Commandments and that Christian placed them in plain sight to laugh at the "zombies" who wouldn't even notice. Supposedly the New World Order elitists are developing a life-extension technology that they don't want to share with, well, us "zombies."

Dice is not alone in his New World Order view. Radio Liberty, a Christian website based in Soquel, California, claims to have found a book in the public library in Elberton, written by the man who called himself R.C. Christian, that says he commissioned the monument in recognition of Thomas

Paine and the occult philosophy he espoused. (Some believe Paine's *The Age of Reason* reflects Paine's desire to destroy the Judeo-Christian beliefs upon which our country is founded.) Radio Liberty surmises that the group that commissioned the Georgia Guidestones is working toward a New World Order, a new world economic system, and a new world spirituality in thrall to dark and sinister forces. According to Radio Liberty, "The message of the American Stonehenge also foreshadowed the current drive for Sustainable Development. Any time you hear the phrase 'Sustainable Development' used, you should substitute the term 'socialism' to be able to understand what is intended."

THE ROSICRUCIAN CONNECTION

Jay Weidner, a former Seattle radio commentator who now tracks down conspiracies, believes Mr. Christian and his associates were Rosicrucians. He said the choice of R. C. Christian paid homage to the legendary fourteenth-century founder of the Rosicrucians, the mythological Christian Rosenkreutz (see Chapter 3).

GET A CLUE!

A *compass rose* is a figure on a map or nautical chart used to display the orientation of the cardinal directions: north, south, east, and west. It is also the term for the graduated markings found on the traditional magnetic compass. The term dates back to the Middle Ages when thirty-two-point compasses first appeared on Arab nautical charts. These compasses were called *wind roses* because cardinal directions were initially based on which way the wind blew. Naming all thirty-two points on the rose is called *boxing the compass*. «

Considered by some to be an authority on the hermetic and alchemical traditions that spawned the Rosicrucians, Weidner believes that for generations the Rosicrucians have been passing down knowledge of a solar cycle that climaxes every 13,000 years. During this culmination, outsize coronal mass ejections are supposed to devastate Earth. Weidner believes the Rosicrucians think we are moving into a stage of planetary chaos, which began with the 2007–08 collapse of the U.S. financial system and will result eventually in major disruptions of oil and food supplies, creating mass riots and ethnic wars worldwide, all leading up to the Big Event on December 21, 2012 (a date also of significance in the Mayan calendar). "They want to get the population down," Weidner says, "and this is what they think will do it. The Georgia Guidestones are there to instruct the survivors."

COULD IT BE TRUE?

To this day, Martin still refuses to reveal the identity of Mr. Christian, but, according to Randall Sullivan of *Wired Magazine*, he has yet to destroy all the records and documents, including letters from Mr. Christian. Those are reportedly stored in the hard-sided case of a 1983 IBM computer that rests in the back of Martin's garage. When asked if he would ever allow those documents to be revealed, Martin noted that he was still honoring Mr. Christian's desire to have the genesis and the meaning of the Georgia Guidestones remain a mystery.

London Bridge

Masons built a variety of impressive monuments and buildings over the millennia. The splendor, magic, and artistic quality of these sites can still be seen in cities and nations all over the world, ranging from grand European castles to the United

States presidential residence, the White House. Arguably one of the most famous mason-built structures is London Bridge, which connects two sides of London over the Thames River.

London Bridge had many incarnations, beginning with a wooden bridge across the Thames built by the Romans in 46 AD. After the Romans departed, the bridge fell into disrepair and was rebuilt a number of times. It wasn't until 1176 during the reign of King Henry II that the masons took on the enormous task of building a more permanent structure. England's first incarnation of the stone-built London Bridge was completed in 1209 and took thirty-three years to construct.

SPANNING THE ARIZONA DESERT

By 1962, largely due to excessive modern day traffic, the bridge began almost literally crumbling—and slowly sinking—into the Thames. With the London government in financial straits, it needed someone willing to buy the crumbling heirloom and remove it. Robert McCulloch, the chairman of McCulloch Oil Corporation and the founder of Lake Havasu City, a resort city in Arizona, purchased London Bridge for $2,460,000, claiming it as "the largest antique" in the world. McCulloch paid an additional $7 million to have the bridge dismantled, shipped to America, and reconstructed in Lake Havasu.

The bridge is 950 feet long and weighs more than 30 tons. Dismantling it proved extremely tedious as workers had to number each stone to ensure that it could be replicated in Arizona. The bridge's parts were initially shipped to Long Beach, California, and then sent on to Lake Havasu.

THE WRONG BRIDGE?

Published reports suggested that Robert McCulloch had been led to believe that he was in fact purchasing the far more famous Tower Bridge (often mistaken for the London Bridge). Those allegations were vehemently denied and discounted by both McCulloch and London's authorities.

The bridge was reconstructed across a boating channel and was finally opened on October 10, 1971, to great enthusiasm. To complement the bridge and draw more tourists, the town constructed a mini village, complete with many Tudor-style structures, which house various shops.

Conclusion: Secret Places Full of Secretive Americans

Our road tour in this chapter has revealed some of the most intriguing spots in America. Many of these places were once upon a time—and often even now remain—the meeting places of secret societies such as the Freemasons. We have always been a citizenry full of secrets, and that has not changed. In the next chapter, we'll examine the secret societies proliferating in today's America.

CHAPTER 12
SECRET SOCIETIES IN AMERICA TODAY

There are a number of secret societies operating in the United States today—with agendas as varied as their members. From exclusive clubs for the very wealthy to clandestine CIA groups, these organizations invite rumor, innuendo, and accusations of dark and evil deeds. Let's take a closer look at some of the most controversial—and potentially subversive.

The Bohemian Club

In July 2000, filmmaker Alex Jones infiltrated a secluded campground near Monte Rio, California, called the Bohemian Grove. This was the meeting place of the Bohemian Club, an elite group of wealthy and influential politicians, corporate CEOs, and entertainment icons, a group that some claim lies at the very heart of a worldwide satanic conspiracy.

That the Bohemian Grove exists is a matter of public record. The group that has met there since 1872 is a secretive organization for the very wealthy, and by just about anyone's standards it's an odd place. For example, there's a forty-five-foot-tall concrete shrine carved in the shape of an owl. The statue looms over an artificial lake. Jones and his cameraman videotaped a ritual in the grove called the Cremation of Care, in which individuals in black hooded robes received an effigy from a ferryman who had made his way across the lake. They placed it on the altar and set it on fire while famous news anchorman Walter Cronkite gave voice to the owl and intoned the ritual.

Every Republican president since Calvin Coolidge (as well as some Democratic presidents) has been a member and watched or participated in this rite. As well, initiates have included leaders ranging from Henry Kissinger to the former head of Proctor & Gamble. To those who accuse the group of being Satanists, the Grove's devotees explain that the club is simply an excuse for the wealthy and famous to gather and relax. The ceremony is a ritual to show that they should burn their cares and woes and enjoy their time in the beautiful surroundings.

Still, this secret gathering of the world's elite for strange ceremonies is seen by some as proof that the world is ruled by Satanists. The theorists fall into two camps. The first, not surprisingly, are Christians with extreme beliefs. To them, Satan is the enemy and the "prince of this world" (John 14:30), so it's not a great leap to think he has a network of mortal agents working in the world for his evil ends. Since he can offer great power (at a great price), it figures that those in power (politically, economically, or in terms of fame and prestige) probably got it by selling their souls.

Others who subscribe to this idea don't focus on the religious aspect of it, but rather link the Bohemian Club to the Illuminati.

Skull and Bones Club

Some believe that Yale University's secret society known as Skull and Bones, whose membership has included many presidents and influential men (including many in the intelligence community), practices occult rituals and indoctrinates future leaders into the satanic conspiracy. The list of so-called Bonesmen includes both George W. Bush and his father, William Howard Taft, William F. Buckley, John Kerry, and many others.

The social club was formed in 1832, and from the beginning membership was limited. Only fifteen seniors are allowed to join each year, which makes the Skull and Bones a very exclusive club, even by Yale's standards. The group's home, a windowless fortress-style building known as the Tomb, is the center of the group's activities. These supposedly range from bizarre rituals involving skulls, bones, and coffins to confessions of sexual activity. This quasi-Masonic organization has been the center of much speculation. Some claim the group is associated with the Illuminati; others say it's the Knights Templar. Some insist they're Satanists.

THE BONES HAVE IT

Rumor has it that George W. Bush's grandfather Prescott Bush and his fellow Bonesmen stole Geronimo's skull and bones from Ft. Sill, Oklahoma, and took them to the Tomb, where they've been displayed in a glass case ever since. As well, there have been rumors that the society has the skull of Pancho Villa.

Opus Dei

"There is just one life, made of flesh and spirit. And it is this life which has to become, in both soul and body, holy and filled with God."
—Saint Josemaria Escriva, founder of Opus Dei

Opus Dei—Latin for "Work of God"—is a conservative Roman Catholic organization founded in 1928 and dedicated to helping the faithful use their normal lives as a holy path to bring them closer to God. Their 87,000-strong membership around the world is mostly comprised of laypeople, 70 percent of whom are married people leading ordinary lives punctuated by prayer, spiritual coaching, devotions, and retreats. The remaining 30 percent mostly live in Opus Dei centers and are celibate. In addition to prayer and coaching, celibate members practice charity, cheerfulness, and corporal mortification designed to discomfort the practitioner. Mortification can run the gamut from sleeping on the floor to wearing the *cilice,* a spiked chain worn around the thigh.

THE WEARING OF THE CILICE

In Dan Brown's *The Da Vinci Code,* the character Silas, described as an Opus Dei monk, wears a crippling cilice with which he tortures himself to the point of drawing blood.

Long a target of controversy, critics have charged Opus Dei of extreme secrecy, right-wing politics, elitism, and misogyny. It's been claimed that members of Opus Dei were supporters of and in some cases participated in repressive governments such as those of Franco in Spain and Pinochet in Chile. Opus Dei itself denies these charges.

OPUS DEI IN AMERICA

There are 3,000 members of Opus Dei in the United States. The organization runs academic, athletic, and spiritual programs, retreat centers, student residences, and schools across the United States, from their New York headquarters to San Francisco, including:

- The Midtown Sports and Cultural Center in Chicago, Illinois
- Lexington College in Chicago, Illinois
- Montrose School in Boston, Massachusetts
- Westfield Residence in Los Angeles, California

The Ku Klux Klan

The original incarnation of the Ku Klux Klan began in Tennessee in 1866, about a year after the end of the Civil War. The KKK was begun by a tiny band of Southern Army officers who continued to oppose the Union victory and the ensuing dismantling of the Confederacy. They were violently opposed to the freeing of the slaves in the southern states and hoped to terrorize African Americans into remaining passive. The spirit of the Klan was further fueled by resentment of business and political interests from the North who were cashing in on the economic opportunities of the reconstruction. The organization quickly gained regional footholds and popular support that spread throughout the Southern states.

KKK FRATERNITY

The name Ku Klux Klan was probably derived from the Greek word *kuklos*, meaning "band," and patterned after the college fraternity Kuklos Adelphon (Band of Brothers) that was founded at the University of North Carolina in 1812 and dissolved during the Civil War.

The Klan attracted a membership that included radical insurgents, malcontents, and outright criminals. Toward the late 1860s, the KKK turned to violent acts of racist domestic terrorism that triggered harsh reactions from civil and military authorities. Civil and social pressures rapidly reduced the attraction of the group, and their de facto leader, Nathan Bedford Forrest, officially disbanded the Klan in 1869. Although Forrest had little actual control over any of the factionalized groups, the KKK of that era was effectively dissolved.

The Klan was restarted in 1915 and grew as white fears of African Americans continued to smolder. In the 1960s, the Klan played a large role in opposing the Civil Rights movements both in Southern states and in some Midwestern states, including Illinois and Indiana. Although today it is widely condemned as a hate group and supporter of terrorism, it continues to flourish in some parts of America, feeding on hate and nourishing bigotry toward African Americans, Jews, Catholics, and immigrants.

The Bilderberg Group

The Bilderberg Group is an invitation-only conference of influential individuals held each year. The first conference, held at the Hotel de Bilderberg in the Netherlands in 1954, gave the group its name. Members of the group, known as Bilderbergers, wield influence in politics, business, and media. They range from foreign policy and military experts to prime ministers and presidents to royalty and international financiers. Most hail from Europe or North America. Donald Rumsfeld, Paul Wolfowitz, Prince Philip and Prince Charles of England, Madeleine Albright, Gerald Ford, Henry Kissinger, David Rockefeller, Pierre Trudeau, Bill and Hillary Clinton, Tony Blair, Otto von Habsburg, Helmut Schmidt, Peter Jennings, and William F. Buckley Jr. have all been members. There are hundreds of members, and not all attend the group's gathering each year.

BILDERBERG'S REPUBLICANS

According to author Mick Farren, most members of the group profess a conservative and staunchly anti-Communist outlook. However, that hasn't stopped some conspiracy theorists from suggesting that their *real* interests are different. Author Phyllis Schlafly postulated that this group controls the modern Republican Party in the United States and uses it to shape policy in favor of the ultrarich and megacorporations. The ideology revealed at Bilderberg conferences remains extremely pro-capitalist, suggesting that the best interests of the common people are served when banking and big business thrive and grow. Members preach capitalism like a religious dogma. New members invited into the group often have high political aspirations. The existing membership determines how well they fit into the organization's worldview—and thus, whether they should be supported or opposed.

No reporters are allowed in Bilderberg conferences, unless they attend as members—though it's not uncommon for leading journalists to belong to the group. Like all other members, these journalists must keep what happens at the meetings in strict confidence. Conspiracy theorists speculate that all manner of dastardly deeds are plotted in these closed-door sessions. However, when Denis Healey, former U.K. Labour chancellor and current Bilderberger, was confronted with the accusations of conspiracy and world domination, he told a reporter that it was "crap."

THE REST OF THE ROUND TABLE

According to some, the Bilderberg Group is just one portion of a larger secret society known as the Round Table, which includes the Committee of 300 (a secret society supposedly founded by the British upper class in the early eighteenth century), the Olympians, and the Illuminati. When financier Cecil Rhodes died in 1902, he left his vast fortune in the hands of the Rothschilds to create the Round Table. Conspiracists suggest that initially it influenced British politics, but eventually it was able to manipulate events all over the world by creating organizations like the Bilderberg Group, the Trilateral Commission, the Club of Rome, and the Council on Foreign Relations. These groups are undoubtedly real and often operate in secrecy, but whether they're the heart of a worldwide conspiracy is another matter altogether.

THE TRILATERAL COMMISSION

The Trilateral Commission is the brainchild of David Rockefeller and first met in 1973. It consists of approximately 300 businesspeople, bankers, and political figures from Europe, the Asia-Pacific region, and North America. Ostensibly, it exists to promote trade and good relations between these three regions. Its ranks have included Jimmy Carter, George Bush Sr., former Senator Lloyd Bentsen, former National Security Advisor Zbigniew Brzezinski, Dick Cheney, Bill Clinton, John Glenn, Henry Kissinger, and many others. In 1975 the Trilateral Commission released a report called the Crisis of Democracy, stating that the United States had an "excess of democracy." Regarding growing democracies and the expansion of the middle class, commission members have said that "order depends on somehow compelling newly mobilized strata to return to a measure of passivity and defeatism . . . ."

THREE-SIDED IS BAD

Some extreme conspiracists have gone so far as to suggest that the very name *Trilateral* is sinister. Trilateral refers to three. And pyramids, of the sort used by the Masons and the Illuminati are . . . three sided.

When Rockefeller created the Trilateral Commission, he was also chairman of the Council on Foreign Relations. The CFR works to influence U.S. foreign policy. Its membership includes intelligence officials, CEOs of multinational corporations, politicians, and some media personalities, and its roll call includes familiar names like Bush, Cheney, and Kissinger as well as John McCain, Colin Powell, and many others.

Mind Kontrol Ultra

A much more secret operation is connected with the U.S. intelligence community. During World War II, the OSS (forerunner of the CIA) began experimenting with different methods to improve interrogation techniques. This research continued after the war, led by the CIA. By the 1950s, however, the idea evolved from getting a prisoner to talk to getting subjects to do whatever they were told—in other words, mind control or, as it became known, "brainwashing." The CIA called this experimental program MKULTRA. This may sound like something from a science fiction movie, but it's not. It's an established fact and one that the CIA has admitted was real.

A CANDIDATE FOR SECRECY

Americans were introduced to the concept of brainwashing by the 1962 thriller *The Manchurian Candidate,* starring Frank Sinatra and Lawrence Harvey. In the movie, Harvey plays an American soldier secretly programmed by Communists to be an assassin.

At the end of World War II, and for a short time thereafter, the United States helped smuggle Nazi scientists out of Germany and into the United States. This program, known as Operation Paperclip, led to many different research projects.

———— GET A CLUE! ————

Kryptos (Greek for "hidden") is the name of an enigmatic sculpture by American artist James Sanborn, one of 500 works of art in the CIA building in Washington, D.C. The sculpture consists of a large S-shaped panel of copper, set on its edge like a curling metal wall. The surface is engraved with nearly 2,000 encoded letters or ciphertext. The artist worked with a retiring CIA employee to create the cryptographic systems used in the sculpture. The artist also placed mysterious symbols on the campus: granite slabs at odd angles, a compass rose, and a magnetic lodestone. The message is divided into four parts.

It's become a bit of a sport to try to decipher the message, which the artist declared is a riddle within a riddle. To date three parts of the cipher have been solved. According to Sanborn, the only person who supposedly was given a key to the riddle was the CIA director William Webster. «

The CIA even pursued some of the behavioral modification techniques used by these nefarious researchers, using experiments begun in the dark confines of concentration camps. Perhaps driven by rumors of Communist mind-control development, programs with names like Project Chatter and Project Artichoke took up brainwashing research where the Nazis had left off. It was, in fact, an escalating mind-control cold war.

HOLY KILLERS

The word *assassin* comes from a sect of Shia Muslims active around 1090 AD called the Hashshashin, who gain the name from their use of the drug hashish. These holy killers, under the influence of drugs, were convinced that if they murdered for Allah, they would be granted special access to heaven.

In 1953, the most infamous and far-reaching program, MKULTRA, began on orders from the then CIA director Allen Dulles. The scientists involved with MKULTRA weren't just interested in interrogation of prisoners but in real mind control—the mass behavioral modification of foreign leaders, enemy troops, and even civilians.

ESCALATING CONTROL TECHNIQUES

CIA scientists frequently used military personnel, prisoners, and mental patients as subjects, as well as unwitting university volunteers. They sometimes conducted their tests in other countries, particularly in areas where there was little chance of intervention.

Under the direction of psychiatrist and chemist Sidney Gottlieb, MKULTRA used drugs, electroshock therapy, radiation, subsonic transmissions, low-frequency radio waves, sensory deprivation, and various psychological techniques to affect behavior modification. And, according to author Kenn Thomas, they even placed mechanical implants directly in the brains of test subjects. They were interested in lowering victims' will, erasing memories, calming aggression, heightening aggression, manipulating actions, and even creating so-called sleeper agents who lived normal lives until "activated" and compelled into service.

THE DIRTY TRICKSTER

While working on MKULTRA projects, chemist Sidney Gottlieb became known as the "Black Sorcerer" and the "Dirty Trickster." He served as the mastermind behind some of the outlandish schemes to eliminate or discredit Fidel Castro, including spraying the leader's belongings with LSD or putting chemicals in his shoes that would make his beard fall out.

MKULTRA mixed in hypnosis and sensory deprivation to create a synthesis of suggestibility for its targets, who were often unaware of what was going on. The CIA scientists discovered some people possessed a far greater vulnerability to their mind control and brainwashing techniques than others. These subjects, according to John Gittinger, an MKULTRA veteran, can receive hypnotic instructions over the television or radio. Memories can be erased, suppressed, altered, or replaced.

THE MICROCHIP DEFENSE

Timothy McVeigh, perpetrator of the Oklahoma City bombing in 1995, claimed to have a microchip implanted in him by the military, either to track him or possibly to control his actions.

MKULTRA officially ended in 1963, but immediately afterward the MKSEARCH program began and carried on the same studies with the same goals. MKSEARCH also investigated various types of nonconventional weapons, including biological and chemical, as well as odder things like using radar waves to assault the minds of the enemy. While it sounds outlandish, apparently it actually works.

BLAME IT ON THE FREEMASONS

According to author Doug Moench, the Freemasons are one of the primary driving forces behind the CIA. And if Masonry's inner circle were really the Illuminati of old, the ability to send mind-controlled infiltrators into other governments and disrupt or even subvert them from within . . . well, that would be right up their alley. And that's exactly what the most extreme fringe of conspiracy theory believes.

MKSEARCH ended in 1973, but most conspiracy researchers believe that behavior modification experiments continue to this day.

WORLD VISION: ANOTHER CIA FRONT

An evangelical, right-wing charitable organization called World Vision has worked as a CIA front for decades, according to writer Fiona Steel. This is interesting because World Vision might have been the conduit through which Jim Jones, the murderous leader of the Jonestown encampment in Guyana, communicated with his CIA superiors while in Guyana (they visited many times). After the massacre of Jones's supporters in 1978, World Vision worked to repopulate Jonestown with mercenaries from Laos who had worked for the CIA during the Vietnam War. But that's not all. World Vision provides us with links to two other well-known possible MKULTRA operatives.

CATCHER IN THE MKULTRA

In the movie *Conspiracy Theory*, Mel Gibson's character, a former MKULTRA subject, is obsessed with *Catcher in the Rye*. Interestingly, author J. D. Salinger worked in military intelligence during World War II.

Mark David Chapman, the assassin of John Lennon, and John Hinckley, Jr., who shot at Ronald Reagan in 1981, at first blush have nothing in common other than being lone nuts obsessed with pop culture icons. But Hinckley's father served as an official in World Vision, and Chapman also worked for the organization. Hinckley's father was a close friend of then vice president George Bush Sr., who had been director of the CIA. Witnesses who saw the men after the crimes were committed described them as glassy-eyed and in a trance. Perhaps hypnotized. Both had copies of *Catcher in the Rye* with them— a detail that would be insignificant except for its sheer improbability. Many conspiracists speculate that the book is some kind of hypnotic trigger used in MKULTRA conditioning.

REMOTE VIEWING
MKULTRA isn't the strangest clandestine government program. That honor would have to go to the Stargate Project. Stargate was the government's attempt to use psychics to spy on the enemy through a technique called *remote viewing*, as described in documents declassified in the 1990s.

Like MKULTRA, it shows that the government is willing to explore all avenues of research, and also like MKULTRA, it came about because the United States was terrified that its enemies might make a breakthrough in some odd but dangerous field before it could.

In the Stargate Project, as many as fourteen different laboratories had agents using clairvoyance or out-of-body techniques to gather information at a distance. These psychics also practiced precognition, allowing them to predict enemy movements and actions before they happened. These techniques may have even been used during the Iranian hostage crisis of 1979–1981.

The actual usefulness and accuracy of the information provided by Stargate remains in question, and the government says that the project is now defunct.

MEN WHO STARE AT STARGATE

The 2009 movie *The Men Who Stare at Goats*, starring George Clooney, dealt with U.S. government programs to use mind control and paranormal and psychic means to attack the enemy.

WHY SOME BELIEVE THE CIA KILLED JFK

American President John F. Kennedy seemed to be skewering the Freemasons when he delivered an address to a gathering of newspaper publishers on April 17, 1961. The full text, available from the Kennedy Library in Massachusetts, shows that, in context, Kennedy was actually criticizing the CIA. This excerpt makes it clear that Kennedy's concern was government, not fraternities:

"The very word 'secrecy' is repugnant in a free and open society; and we are as a people inherently and historically opposed to secret societies, to secret oaths and to secret proceedings. We decided long ago that the dangers of excessive and unwarranted concealment of pertinent facts far outweighed the dangers which are cited to justify it. Even today, there is little value in opposing the threat of a closed society by imitating its arbitrary restrictions. Even today, there is little value in insuring the survival of our nation if our traditions do not survive with it. And there is very grave danger that an announced need for increased security will be seized upon by those anxious to expand its meaning to the very limits of official censorship and concealment. That I do not intend to permit to the extent that it is in my control. And no official of my Administration, whether his rank is high or low, civilian or military, should interpret my words here tonight as an excuse to censor the news, to stifle dissent, to cover up our mistakes or to withhold from the press and the public the facts they deserve to know."

Conclusion: Secret Societies Forever

As we've seen in this chapter, humans' affinity for secret societies is as strong today as it was in ancient times. Sometimes these clandestine organizations are modeled after the Ancient Mystery Schools, and they share the desire to seek the Divine Truth and Light. Others are perversions of the Ancient Mysteries, operating out of greed and lust or power rather than the enlightenment of humankind.

But as we'll see in Chapter 13, our quest for a better society inspired by knowledge, truth, and beauty is alive and well and dedicated to the noetic sciences.

CHAPTER 13

BACK TO THE FUTURE: THE NOETICS INSTITUTE

In Dan Brown's *The Lost Symbol*, symbologist Robert Langdon forms an alliance with Peter Solomon's beautiful and accomplished sister, Dr. Katherine Solomon. The doctor, who turns out to be a wealth of information on the secrets of Washington, D.C., as well as a hottie, is a researcher in noetic science. She maintains a secret laboratory in Washington, hidden in the depths of an enormous "pod," a building as large as a football field that contains such wonders as a giant squid. And, she tells Langdon, her research is poised on the edge of a breakthrough, a discovery that will "change everything."

Although no such noetic sciences laboratory exists in the nation's capital—at least, not that we know of—the noetic sciences are real and are being studied in this country and abroad. In fact, in Petaluma, California, on a 200-acre compound, there exists the Institute of Noetic Sciences that, with the publication of Brown's book, suddenly found itself catapulted into the public light.

What Is Noetics?

The word *noetic* comes from the Greek word *noetikos*, meaning "mental" or "thought." Broadly, the noetic sciences are concerned with studying nonrational ways of knowing things and with the relationship between body and mind. In particular, those involved in the noetic sciences want to find out how to use the mind to affect the body and to tap into hitherto unused abilities.

The institute in Petaluma began in the 1970s and was founded by an astronaut named Edgar Mitchell. Mitchell was part of the Apollo space program and was the sixth person to walk on the surface of the moon. While on the lunar mission, he saw Earth rising over the surface of the moon. The experience, according to him, was profoundly moving and spiritually enlightening: "The presence of divinity became almost palpable, and I knew that life in the universe was not just an accident based on random processes. . . . The knowledge came to me directly." Mitchell realized at that moment that traditional science, in which he'd been trained, couldn't deal with the spiritual structure of reality. Mitchell, upon his return, wrote a book about his experience, *The Way of the Explorer: An Astronaut's Journey Through the Material and Mystical Worlds*.

The astronaut became more and more convinced that the traditional sciences in which he'd been grounded couldn't explain the spiritual transformation he experienced while watching Earth rise. The mind, he came to believe, is capable of changing and affecting matter, including the body in which it resides. Mitchell received further proof of the powers of the mind when his kidney cancer was successfully treated at a distance by a teenage healer living in Vancouver.

We Are Not Alone

Mitchell's experiences on the moon and his spiritual awakening also opened him to suggestions that the human race is not alone in the universe. Mitchell became convinced that humans have been visited by beings from outer space and that these visitors are attempting to establish contact with us.

This isn't an unusual viewpoint, of course, and many others have made similar claims. The Roswell Incident of 1947 provides some of the most convincing evidence that Mitchell may be right. In July of that year, a farmer near Roswell found strange debris in his field. When he told the authorities, the military arrived to investigate. They hauled away the debris, and several weeks later the Roswell Army Air Field issued a press release stating that they had recovered a crashed flying disc. Later that day, the Air Force corrected its announcement, saying that it had recovered a weather balloon, not a flying saucer. And thus began sixty years of argument. The Air Force forbade any photographs of the "weather balloon" and tried to limit the story. But it was too late.

Although many initially dismissed the Roswell story as a hoax, others were willing to believe that something strange had happened, something the military was covering up. Edgar Mitchell, although skeptical for many years of such claims, eventually came to believe them.

Together with Paul Temple, Mitchell helped found the Institute of Noetic Sciences in 1973. Today the institute occupies buildings that include assembly halls, a meditation center, and housing for visitors. It has published two journals, *Noetics* and *Shift: At the Frontiers of Consciousness*, though both have been suspended, as well as a number of books. The institute's mission is to "advance the science of consciousness and human experience to serve individual and collective transformation."

Healing the Body with the Mind

In *The Lost Symbol*, Katherine Solomon is preoccupied with such problems as whether or not there is such a thing as a human soul and if it can be measured in some fashion. She conducts an experiment in which she weighs a man just before and just after his death and detects a small, almost imperceptible difference. Her conclusion is that this difference is the weight of his soul.

The Institute for Noetic Sciences hasn't done any such experiments. Instead, they are preoccupied with issues such as the ability of humans to affect matter at a distance, the efficacy of prayer, the validity of astrology and nontraditional approaches to knowledge (for instance, channeling), and psychic healing.

Their researchers believe that, in the words of one of their elder statesmen, Willis Harman, "In some sense much more fundamental than is implied in conventional psychology, our belief systems create our reality." If the mind can be sufficiently trained, it can directly affect the body, transforming cancerous cells into healthy ones, destroying infectious diseases, and prolonging life while expanding consciousness.

Some of the researchers at the institute and elsewhere argue that the mind's ability to do this grows directly from its connection with a universal awareness. This is a bit like the Force in *Star Wars* but on a higher and more profound level. In her book *Fingerprints of God: The Search for the Science of Spirituality*, Barbara Bradley Haggerty argues that the universe is entangled together, knit into one by a kind of universal consciousness. This isn't God necessarily — not all researchers believe this consciousness has a purpose or imposes any moral order on the universe. But it binds all living things together.

Rationalism Versus Mysticism

The kinds of abilities that students of the noetic sciences are searching for are not new to the human race. Often, researchers suggest, the key to understanding our higher consciousness can be found in ancient wisdom. In the 1970s and 1980s, such books as Fritjof Capra's *The Tao of Physics* and Gary Zukav's *The Dancing Wu Li Masters* explored the implications of quantum physics, which often seemed to defy rationality, and traced explanations for these phenomena to the writings of ancient sages in China.

Quantum physics, for example, says that the very act of *observing* matter on a subatomic level *changes* it. Capra, Zukav, and modern followers of noetic science point to this as an example of the ability of consciousness to change things. They argue that consciousness is something that exists apart from the body and can directly affect the reality around it. Thought is capable of transforming matter.

Capra and Zukav argued that the key to understanding such things lay in uniting the discoveries of quantum physics with traditional mystical texts, usually dismissed by scientists as religion. Followers of noetics suggested that there can be a unity between the two approaches. Some researchers have even suggested that Jesus' "miracles" were, in fact, examples of Jesus using his consciousness to affect reality—for instance when he changed water into wine or told his followers that with their faith they could move mountains.

Western science, with its emphasis on rationalism and "fact" discounted the unity of mind and body. Following the approach of Rene Descartes in the seventeenth century, science and philosophy split mind and matter into two parts, often at war with one another. Noetics is a means of reuniting the two, making each of them stronger as they work in tandem. The unity of mind and body is key to unlocking our abilities and to finding a road to personal and social transformation. This is what Katherine Solomon meant when she told Robert Langdon that her research would change everything.

APPENDIX A
RECOMMENDED READING

Baigent, Michael, Henry Lincoln, Richard Leigh. *Holy Blood, Holy Grail*. Dell, reissue edition, 1983.

Brown, Dan. *The Da Vinci Code*. Doubleday, New York, a division of Random House, Inc. 2003.

Bullock, Stephen C. "The Revolutionary Transformation of American Freemasonry," 1752-1792, *William and Mary Quarterly* 37, 1990.

Claudy, Carl H. *Introduction to Freemasonry I: Entered Apprentice*. The Temple Publishers, Washington, D.C., 1931.

Claudy, Carl H. *Introduction to Freemasonry II: Fellowcraft*. The Temple Publishers, Washington, D.C., 1931.

Claudy, Carl H. *Introduction to Freemasonry III: Master Mason*. The Temple Publishers, Washington, D.C., 1931.

Clausen, Henry C. 33°, Sovereign Grand Commander. *Clausen's Commentaries on Morals and Dogma*. Supreme Council,

33rd Degree, Ancient and Accepted Scottish Rite of Freemasonry, Southern Jurisdiction, Washington D.C. 1974, 1976.

Coil, Henry Wilson. *Coil's Masonic Encyclopedia.* Macoy Pub & Masonic Supply Co., 1996

Cornwell, Patricia. *Portrait Of A Killer: Jack The Ripper—Case Closed.* Berkeley True Crime, 2003.

de Hoyos, Arturo and S. Brent Morris. *Is it True What they Say About Freemasonry?* M. Evans and Company, Inc., New York, 2004.

Hunter, Frederick M. *The Regius Manuscript.* Research Lodge of Oregon, No.198, Portland Oregon, 1952.

Jacob, Margaret C. *Living the Enlightenment: Freemasonry and Politics in Eighteenth-Century Europe.* Oxford University Press, New York, 1991.

Jeffers, Paul. *Freemasons: Inside the World's Oldest Secret Society.* Citadel Press Books. Kensington Publishing Corp, 2005.

Knight, Christopher, and Robert Lomas. *The Hiram Key.* Fair Winds Press, Gloucester, Massachusetts, 1996.

Knight, Christopher, and Robert Lomas. *The Book of Hiram: Freemasonry, Venus, and the Secret Key to the Life of Jesus.* Element, an imprint of HarperCollins Publishers, Hammersmith, London, 2003.

Knight, Christopher, and Robert Lomas. *Uriel's Machine*. Fair Winds Press, Gloucester, Massachusetts, 2001.

Knight, Stephen. *Jack the Ripper: The Final Solution*. David McKay Co., 1976.

Knight, Stephen. *The Brotherhood: The Secret World of The Freemasons*. Dorset Press, 1986.

Lomas, Robert. *Freemasonry & the Birth of Modern Science*. Fairwinds Press, 2003

Mackey, Albert Gallatin. *The History of Freemasonry; Its Legendary Origins*. Random House Value Publishing, 1966.

Mackey's Revised *Encyclopedia of Freemasonry*. The Masonic History Company, 1912.

MacNulty, Kirk. *Freemasonry: A Journey Through Ritual and Symbol*. Thames and Hudson, 1991

Macoy, Robert. *A Dictionary of Freemasonry*. Gramercy Books, Random House Value Publishing, 2000.

Naudon, Paul. *The Secret History of Freemasonry: Its Origins and Connection to the Knights Templar*. Inner Traditions, Rochester, Vermont, 1991.

Newton, Joseph F. *The Builders*. The Supreme Council, 33rd Degree, A.A.S.R., Lexington Massachusetts, 1973.

Pike, Albert. *Morals and Dogma*. Kessinger Publishing, 2004.

Ridley, Jasper. *The Freemasons: A History of the World's Most Powerful Secret Society*. Arcade Publishing, Inc. New York. 1999, 2001.

Roberts, Allen E. *Freemasonry in American History*. Macoy Publishing and Masonic Supply Co., Inc., Richmond Virginia, 1985.

Robinson, John J. *Born in Blood: The Lost Secrets of Freemasonry*. M. Evans and Company, Inc., New York, 1989.

Rumbelow, Donald. *The Complete Jack the Ripper*. Little Brown & Co., 1975.

Short, Martin. *Inside the Brotherhood: Further Secrets of the Freemasons*. Dorset Press, 1990.

Young, John K. *Sacred Sites of the Knights Templar*. Fair Winds Press, Gloucester, Massachusetts, 2003.

APPENDIX B
GLOSSARY

Albert Pike
The Sovereign Grand Commander of the Southern Supreme Council of the Scottish Rite from 1859 to 1891.

Ancient Arabic Nobles of the Mystic Shrine
The most visible body of Freemasonry, commonly referred to as Shriners.

Blue Lodge
One of the most commonly used terms in Freemasonry for lodges conferring the first three degrees. It is primarily used in the United States and Canada.

Cable Tow
Also a measure of distance, it symbolically binds each Mason to all of his brethren. The tie is as strong and lengthy as an initiate and the abilities he brings to the Craft.

Chapter of the Rose Croix
The second division of the Scottish Rite system that includes the fifteenth through eighteenth degrees.

Circumnabulation
In a lodge there is a central object or point (an altar), which the initiate must walk around. This ancient practice is meant to show that an initiate is prepared to embark on his fraternal journey.

Commanderies of Knights Templar
Also called Chivalric Masonry, it includes three orders including the Illustrious Order of the Red Cross, the Order of Malta, and the Order of the Temple.

Compass
One of the most important and prominent symbols of Freemasonry, it represents virtue as a measure of one's life and conduct. It also signifies restraint, skill, and knowledge.

Consistory Degrees
The fourth and final division of the Scottish Rite system which includes the thirty-first and thirty-second degrees. The thirty-third degree, though part of the Consistory, is honorary.

Council of Cryptic Masonry
Often called Cryptic Masonry, it is the second body of the York Rite which confers three degrees including Royal Master, Select Master, and Super Excellent Master.

Council of Kadosh
The third division of the Scottish Rite system which includes the nineteenth through thirtieth degrees.

Craft
A common term which simply refers to Freemasonry.

Degree
A level of Freemasonry to which individuals can ascend.

Entered Apprentice
The first degree of Craft Masonry where an initiate is introduced to the Craft. It symbolizes an individual's spiritual

birth into the fraternity, and begins his quest for "light," or knowledge.

Fellowcraft
The second degree of Craft Masonry which signifies an initiate's adult phase into the Craft where he seeks to acquire the knowledge and spiritual tools necessary to build character and improve society.

Four Cardinal Virtues
Temperance, fortitude, prudence, and justice.

"G," the Letter
Symbolically it stands for geometry or God. It also commonly refers to God as the Grand Architect of the Universe or Grand Master of the Universe.

Grand Lodge
The governing body which oversees all regular lodges under its jurisdiction.

Grand Lodge of England
The first Grand Lodge formed in 1717, when four lodges united in England. It is generally accepted that this marked the start of organized Freemasonry.

Grand Master
The highest ranking individual of a Grand Lodge. It is an elected position and one of great prestige within the Craft.

Hiram Abiff
The architect and Master Mason who oversaw the building of the Temple of Solomon. His legend is referred to throughout Freemasonry.

Hoodwinked
Initiates to the Craft are hoodwinked, or blindfolded, which represents the veil of silence and secrecy that surrounds the mysteries of Freemasonry.

Knights Templar
A military and religious order of warrior monks founded in 1118 by French Knight Hughes de Payens. The Templars fought during the Crusades.

Lodge
A two-fold term referring to both a group of Masons and the building in which they meet. Masonic buildings are often called temples.

Lodge of Perfection
The first division of the Scottish Rite system which includes the fourth through fourteenth degrees. Usually referred to as "ineffable" degrees.

Master Mason
The third degree of Craft Masonry which symbolically links a Mason's soul and his own inner nature and belief system.

Operative Masonry
Operative refers to stonemasons who were part of the actual trade.

Order of the Eastern Star
The world's largest fraternal organization whose members include both men and women. Their order includes over a million individuals worldwide.

Pillars on the Porch
Symbolically linked to Solomon's Temple, they stand at the entrance to the Temple. The left pillar is called Boaz, and the right is named Jachin.

Royal Arch Chapter
Part of the York Rite, Royal Arch Masonry consists of four degrees, including Mark Master, Past Master Most Excellent Master, and Royal Arch.

Scottish Rite
A concordant body of Freemasonry, it offers thirty-three additional degrees. Also called the Ancient and Accepted Scottish Rite.

Speculative Masonry
Speculative refers to Freemasons who were not part of the actual trade of masonry.

Square
One of the most prominent symbols of Freemasonry, it represents morality and truthfulness.

Supreme Being
The Masonic reference to Deity. Given that Masonry is non-sectarian, each Mason's Supreme Being is different. The more commonly used term among the brethren is Grand Architect of the Universe.

Thirty-Third Degree Mason
One who has completed the first three degrees of Craft Masonry and the thirty-two degrees of the Scottish Rite. The thirty-third degree is honorary and the candidate must be voted upon.

Three Great Lights of Masonry
The square, compass, and Volume of the Sacred Law.

United Grand Lodge of England
The union of two Grand Lodges in Britain in 1813. Today the Lodge is formally known as the United Grand Lodge of Free and Accepted Masons of England, and informally called the United Grand Lodge of England.

Volume of the Sacred Law
The most prominent of the Three Great Lights. Members of the Craft practice many different religions, so the sacred text of choice varies. In general, it is the Holy Bible.

Working Tools
Each degree of Masonry has certain symbolism associated with its level which represent the morals and forces necessary in building and rebuilding the nature of humankind.

Worshipful Master
The highest ranking member of a lodge or blue lodge. Also called a Right Worshipful Master. He is elected and serves a one-year term.

York Rite
A concordant body of Freemasonry originating from the English city of York. It offers additional degrees within its three bodies—the Royal Arch Chapter, Council of Cryptic Masonry, and Commanderies of Knights Templar.

INDEX